Alicia Britt Chole has an eloquence and thoughtfulness with words that are a rare gift. Her writings have deeply influenced me and I keep going back to them again and again. This devotional will provide Christ-followers everywhere a rich experience through the Lenten season. Her insights will help you linger over the sayings of Jesus and, more importantly, help you love Jesus more deeply.

—LANCE WITT
FOUNDER OF REPLENISH MINISTRIES

My dearest friend Alicia has done it again. And this time bringing our thoughts and attention to our interior life as we journey through Lent together. She writes with her whole heart laid bare…intuitive, prophetic, and profoundly inspiring, calling forth a revolution of soul health, stirring our passion to know Jesus more.

—DARLENE ZSCHECH
COMPOSER, WORSHIP LEADER, PASTOR, AND SPEAKER

Once again, God has sounded a clear chord of revelation through Alicia Chole. In her book, *40 Days of Decrease*, God uses her to lovingly guide the reader into recognizing His presence, purpose, and power in times of necessary loss. Against a backdrop of societal belief that identifies God in terms of individual gain and increase, Chole alerts and encourages us to recognize God's will and ways in the midst of experiencing personal reduction. In so doing, she leads us into a fast that further conforms us into the image of Christ. God has entrusted Alicia with a gift rare and precious in nature.

—DR. CLAUDE R. ALEXANDER, JR.
LEAD PASTOR OF THE PARK BAPTIST CHURCH, CHARLOTTE, NC

This book is a breath of fresh air. In a world where the loudest voices seem to all say that fulfillment is only found in addition, Alicia Britt Chole beckons us to reacquaint ourselves with the power of subtraction. *40 Days of Decrease* is a beautiful invitation to prepare for the celebration of Jesus' resurrection in a more meaningful way than ever before.

—DAVID LINDELL
LEAD CAMPUS PASTOR, JAMES RIVER CHURCH WEST

More than ever I am persuaded that the true purpose of Christian spiritual formation is not self-help or even spiritual growth, but loving God and serving God's world. Christ-followers are hungry for the kind of Lenten fast that sets us free to love and serve…and Alicia's creation is a powerful tool to lead us on that journey.

—DR. DAN BRUNNER
PROFESSOR OF CHRISTIAN HISTORY AND FORMATION,
GEORGE FOX EVANGELICAL SEMINARY

Alicia is brutally honest; she's true; she is much closer to the Jesus path, the downward journey to the cross, than the surplus of tepid and painless "American-Christianity-lite." Hers are stern, robust and healing words, ideas, paragraphs, days. Alicia is not a pseudo-martyr, simply inviting us to wallow in (or idolize) her pain and sadness. Rather, through the delicate turn of the word, idea and phrase, she invites us to walk with Jesus Himself (not with her), to join her and others on the tough and true journey of transformational discipleship. This is the diet of true Christian Lent (You will learn more about Lent than ever before!), crucial for those who prefer to jump over the 40 days and land immediately into an exciting resurrection Sunday. I myself need this deep and disturbing book.

—DR. WILLIAM D. TAYLOR
SENIOR MENTOR, WORLD EVANGELICAL ASSOCIATION

Alicia does something quite remarkable with this book. Her gentle and poetic prose invites us to forgo life's clutter and heavy burdens, leading us to joy and freedom of a deeper life with God. So practical. So helpful.

—DR. NATHAN FOSTER
AUTHOR OF *THE MAKING OF AN ORDINARY SAINT*

I am continually stunned by Alicia's vivid conciseness, which cuts quickly to the unseen core of carnality. She settles down the reader into the joy of purposeful brokenness. This devotional is more than a "must-read;" it gripped my heart as a "must-experience."

—DR. DAVID J. NIQUETTE
LEAD PASTOR OF CHRIST CENTER COMMUNITY CHURCH, FORT COLLINS, CO

PRAISE FOR *40 DAYS OF DECREASE*

Alicia has a unique way of framing truth. Her heartfelt and thoughtful words penetrate the soul and make you feel and think in new ways.

—MARK BATTERSON
LEAD PASTOR, NATIONAL COMMUNITY CHURCH, WASHINGTON, D.C.

I shared the platform with Alicia, heard her speak and realized how much she loved the Lord and His Word. I was taken by this dear woman.

—KAY ARTHUR
INTERNATIONAL BIBLE TEACHER, CO-FOUNDER OF PRECEPT MINISTRIES

Alicia has written a beautiful Lenten devotional, filled with gems that will draw your soul to God and His love. I highly recommend it!

—PETER SCAZZERO
PASTOR AND BESTSELLING AUTHOR OF *EMOTIONALLY HEALTHY SPIRITUALITY*

I have always loved Alicia's writing and I am falling deeper for her prose bathed in prophetic realism. She refuses to be sentimental and forces the reader to find a gritty Gospel where life, pain, and redemption live in the same space. The majority of writers claiming a spiritual center serve up prosaic prose, peppered with simple and cute couplets of sanitized faith, but Alicia delves into what Howard Thurman calls "the altar on the island of the soul." This is the kind of writing that cuts and heals. Bravo!

—DR. OTIS MOSS, III
SENIOR PASTOR, TRINITY UNITED CHURCH OF CHRIST, CHICAGO, IL

I first encountered Alicia Britt Chole through her profound book, *Anonymous*, and I am delighted to see this new companion to nurturing our life together in the Spirit. *40 Days of Decrease* is a unique and original approach to the traditional preparation for the climax of Easter. The daily Reflection and Today's Fast components are gems, and the 40 distinct fasts she proposes offer a transformational praxis that redefines the meaning of hunger.

—DR. KEN BOA
PRESIDENT OF REFLECTIONS MINISTRIES, AUTHOR OF *CONFORMED TO HIS IMAGE*

Alicia Britt Chole's book is a wonderful journey into the purpose and heart of the Lenten season for those who may not be familiar with it. As someone who grew up in a non-liturgical church context, I never understood how to engage Lent as a sacred act of decreasing self and elevating Christ. Alicia's profound yet accessible revelation of decreasing ourselves so that Christ might increase in our lives will bless both seasoned participants in Lent and those who are just beginning to express this powerful spiritual discipline.

—KERRI WEEMS

AUTHOR OF *RHYTHMS OF GRACE: DISCOVERING GOD'S TEMPO FOR YOUR LIFE*

To me, Alicia is the complete package. Who I see day in and day out is the same person I see in public—a true follower of Jesus.

—DR. BARRY JAY CHOLE

CO-FOUNDER OF LEADERSHIP INVESTMENT INTENSIVES, ALICIA'S HUSBAND

Alicia has a tremendous passion to communicate the wholeness of God's purpose for broken people in broken communities, and shine a light on that path to wholeness and peace.

—SARA GROVES

AUTHOR, RECORDING ARTIST

Alicia is a dynamic sage and spiritual guide for the twenty-first-century seeker of God.

—DR. FRANK ANTHONY THOMAS

PROFESSOR OF HOMILETICS AT CHRISTIAN THEOLOGICAL SEMINARY

In her beautifully transparent way, Alicia walks us through her journey toward utter dependence on Jesus and guides us in how to do the same. You will be blessed by her story and encouraged to look at fasting in a whole new way during this forty-day study. She will teach you how to rest in the promise that where He calls, He blesses and restores.

—JENNIFER ROTHSCHILD

AUTHOR OF *INVISIBLE: HOW YOU FEEL IS NOT WHO YOU ARE*, FOUNDER OF FRESH GROUNDED FAITH EVENTS AND WOMENSMINISTRY.NET

40 DAYS OF DECREASE

40 DAYS OF DECREASE

A Different Kind of Hunger. A Different Kind of Fast.

Alicia Britt Chole

W PUBLISHING GROUP

AN IMPRINT OF THOMAS NELSON

Published in Nashville, Tennessee, by W Publishing, an imprint of Thomas Nelson. W Publishing and Thomas Nelson are registered trademarks of HarperCollins Christian Publishing, Inc.

Thomas Nelson titles may be purchased in bulk for educational, business, fund-raising, or sales promotional use. For information, please e-mail SpecialMarkets@ThomasNelson.com.

Unless otherwise noted, Scripture references are taken from the Holy Bible, New International Version®, NIV®. Copyright © 1973, 1978, 1984, 2011 by Biblica, Inc.™ Used by permission of Zondervan. All rights reserved worldwide. www.zondervan.com. The "NIV" and "New International Version" are trademarks registered in the United States Patent and Trademark Office by Biblica, Inc.™

Scripture quotations marked NASB are taken from the New American Standard Bible®, Copyright © 1960, 1962, 1963, 1968, 1971, 1972, 1973, 1975, 1977, 1995 by The Lockman Foundation. Used by permission. (www.Lockman.org)

Library of Congress Cataloging-in-Publication Data

Chole, Alicia Britt.
   40 days of decrease: A different kind of hunger. A different kind of fast. / Alicia Britt Chole.
    pages cm
   ISBN 978-0-7180-7660-3 (trade paper)
   1. Lent—Meditations. I. Title. II. Title: Forty days of decrease.
   BV85.C495 2016
   242'.34—dc23
   2015020807

Printed in the United States of America

19 20 21 LSC 14 13 12 11

To my eldest, Jonathan, whose life is a gift from God.
Jonathan, a long time ago you and I were sitting together one night
near a bonfire and you asked me a weighty question that at its core was
about decrease. "Mom," you began, looking deeply into my eyes, "will
you die one day?" "Yes, my love," I replied. "One day Mommy will die."
You breathed in my words and began to walk and walk, processing
mysteries of faith with your golden mind and soul. Then you
announced, "Mom, it's okay. It's okay if you die one day. Jesus can take
you to heaven. BUT, I'm going to be the one who carries you there."
One day, my beloved son, my decrease on earth will be complete. On
that day, rest assured that your love truly helped carry me to heaven.
I pray that I will be able to read this book to you for decades to
come. But if you ever find yourself absent my voice, may these
words guide you into Jesus' arms. (I will be waiting for you there.)

CONTENTS

CONTENTS

PROLOGUE

THE GRAND REDUCTION

The sabbatical started more suddenly and violently than anticipated. A high fever, a few scans, multiple masses, possibly a lethal abscess ... the specialists convened, conferred, counseled me to cancel all engagements, and began cutting.

The reduction had begun.

Waking from surgery, my first memory was seeing a dear friend place a hand over her mouth. Later she told me, "I'd never seen anyone that color, alive." The masses, thankfully, were all benign. But my body did not respond well to the invasion. The area's organs went into hibernation and for the first time in my life, I became familiar with breathtaking *pain*.

The experience redefined that word for me. It hurt to be awake. It hurt to see my children's fear. It hurt to hear, "We don't know why." In time, it would even hurt to hope. Reductions, it seems, have blurry release dates. Days stacked upon one another in vain like whisper-thin blankets with no warmth to offer. Though technology blinked, beeped, and buzzed noisily around me, the organs slept on. This healing simply would not be hurried. The wound was evidently too great to risk haste.

After eight days in the hospital, the doctors sent me home. "At this point, I give you a fifty-fifty chance that the organs will come back online," the specialist offered. With those words, my entire recovery-time "to do" list vaporized in the desert heat of pain. All I could do was sit and be loved—a need that my family filled extravagantly. Little did I know that the pain was under assignment: it was making room in my life for another operation well beyond the reach of any surgeon's scalpel.

I would not trade that desert of pain for the world.

Deserts unclutter the soul. The hot desert sun vaporizes all manner of luxuries. Then the cold, shelterless nights expose the essential guts of life. I needed to eat, to sleep, to be protected, and to not be alone. Lent had come half a year early. God asked me to fast mental and physical strength. He invited me into holy weakness.

I found Jesus there.

We often think of Jesus' fast beginning when He stepped into the Judean wilderness. But the fast actually began three decades earlier when the Glory of heaven was wrapped in plain paper and given as a gift to mankind.

The Grand Reduction had begun.

Jesus fasted omnipresence and clothed Himself with flesh. He fasted being worshiped by angels and accepted the disregard of man. He fasted the Voice that birthed planets and submitted to the silence of thirty hidden years:

How must it have felt—knowing he had the power to heal—to have to walk past children suffering with leprosy? What would it have been like—knowing that his conception was miraculous—to be unable to defend his mother when others whispered about her past? And how agonizing would it be—when his Word could one day raise the dead to life again—to stand by while those he loved (perhaps even Joseph his father) died?[1]

We are duly thankful, challenged, and inspired by Jesus' forty-day fast from food in the Judean wilderness. Perhaps we should likewise be grateful, awed, and humbled by His thirty-year fast from praise, power, and potential in Nazareth.

It takes a great deal of strength to choose weakness.

Jesus chose voluntarily. I did not possess the courage or wisdom to volunteer. So God, for the sake of my soul, took me there involuntarily. His drafts are merciful indeed.

When He calls us to fast strength—when He drafts us into decrease—God's purposes are clear:

> Remember how the LORD your God led you all the way in the wilderness these forty years, to humble you and to test you in order to know what was in your heart, whether or not you would keep his commands. He humbled you, causing you to hunger and then feeding you with manna, which neither you nor your ancestors had known, to teach you that man does not live on bread alone but on every word that comes from the mouth of the LORD. (Deuteronomy 8:2–3)

To humble us, to test us, to know what is in our hearts . . . such is the sifting power of helplessness. In our daily lives, we may prefer self-reliance. But perhaps utter dependence is the truer friend of our souls.

Two weeks past the surgery, I picked up my journal and wrote, "I used to think I could do just about anything. Now I know I can't." Through the fasting of strength, God was "causing me to hunger." Helplessness exposed the contents of my heart. God began to feed me.

As He nourished me, my eyes were opened to see an invisible danger that had been growing within me. Prior to surgery, God was not absent. The challenge was that self was so very present. Though I had purposed to live simply, clutter was collecting around my faith. I was becoming more vulnerable to sin, but sin of a slightly different strain than in earlier years.

We all guard against sins of commission and we are vigilant toward sins of omission. But achievements—even in small doses—can make us vulnerable to sins of *addition*: adding niceties and luxuries to our list of basic needs, adding imaginations onto the strong back of vision, adding self-satisfaction to the purity of peace.

Jesus emerged from His thirty-year fast armored to resist such sins of addition. He walked into the Judean desert and with each "It is written" affirmed the sacredness of decrease. He walked out of the Judean desert and with each step fulfilled His calling without compromise. Jesus lived a truly uncluttered life and died a focused, eternally fruitful death. How I long to follow His example.

Years later, the pain from that surgery has, thankfully, disappeared. The fruit of pain's assignment in my soul has, thankfully, remained. My desert decrease was divine. May this season of preparation provide us the opportunity to pause and be grateful for reductions. Ultimately we are grateful for the Grand Reduction, when Jesus came from heaven to earth and from earth to the cross. But we can also be thankful for the lesser reductions, when God drafts us into deserts.

Throughout our collective *40 Days of Decrease*, let us rest assured that when Father God calls us to fast increase, decrease will purify our souls.

INTRODUCTION

What might be the fruit of fasting stinginess? What would happen if our churches fasted spectatorship? What might occur if our families fasted accumulation? What could change if our offices fasted revisionism? What might erupt if a new generation fasted escapism? Such fasts could trigger a spiritual revolution.

40 Days of Decrease guides readers through a study of Jesus' uncommon and uncomfortable call to abandon the world's illusions, embrace His kingdom's realities, and journey cross-ward and beyond. Designed to prepare our hearts for Easter, *40 Days of Decrease* can also be experienced by those who desire to honor Christ's resurrection year-round. A life-engaging guide for communities and individuals, each day of *40 Days of Decrease* features a devotional based upon Jesus' life, guidance for reflection, suggested (and occasionally surprising) daily fasts, an inspiring quote for prayerful meditation, an optional and somewhat academic sidebar chronicling the historical development, practices, and images of Lent, and a suggested Scripture reading with journaling space.

As you begin your experience, consider setting aside thirty minutes or an hour every morning to read, reflect, and prepare your heart for that day's fast. Though each fast could theme an entire week or month, in *40 Days of Decrease* I offer forty different fasts in the hope that collectively they will prepare us to be duly awed by Christ's resurrection by being duly available to daily crucifixion. With carefully selected quotes from Jesus-centric traditions and readings crafted to engage our modern minds with the most disenchanting days of the first disciples' lives, *40 Days of Decrease* seeks to reintroduce Lent as a wise mentor that encourages us to reframe unanswered questions, darker seasons, and spiritual disillusionment as the shedding of earthly illusions and the gaining of God's reality.

In Protestant and Catholic traditions, the counting of Lent's forty days excludes Sundays.[1] Likewise, *40 Days of Decrease* offers readings and exercises exclusive of Sundays for six days a week, beginning with Ash Wednesday.[2] As we experience this sacred season and the holiness of loss and less in Jesus' journey cross-ward, may our hearts open vulnerably to a greater commitment to love and be loved by the Savior. For, in the words of Orthodox Reverend Alexander Schmemann, "The purpose of Lent is not to force on us a few formal obligations, but to 'soften' our heart so that it may open itself to the realities of the spirit, to experience the hidden 'thirst and hunger' for communion with God."[3]

Let such softening begin!

DAY ONE

We ache deep within to meaningfully honor Christ's resurrection. Yet, in practice, this focal point in the liturgical calendar is often a celebration of *public holiday* more than it is of *humanity's hope*. At day's end, we fall asleep well fed and perhaps even grateful, yet still somehow something short of *awed*. Inspired by the church's ancient tradition of Lent, we then add discipline to the celebration, voluntarily adopting a form of temporary discomfort to self with the intention of bringing to mind the discomfort of the cross (which is unspeakable). And still, our twenty-first-century discomfort remains mild and our first-century remembrance remains meager.

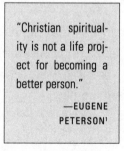

"Christian spirituality is not a life project for becoming a better person."

—EUGENE PETERSON[1]

Though what is specifically "given up for Lent" shifts from generation to generation, the broad categories of entertainment, pleasure, and food have remained constant through the centuries. Caffeine, chocolate, designer coffee, carbs, and social media currently rank among the more popular offerings. In an age suffocating in self, any willful fast from what much of the planet would deem a luxury is to be commended. However, since commendation cannot be confused with preparation, I must ask: can such polite fasts alone truly prepare us to be awed by Christ's resurrection?

In English, the Latin *Mortem tuam annuntiámus, Dómine, et tuam resurrectiónem confitémur, donec vénias* is translated as, "Your death we proclaim, Lord, and your resurrection we confess, until you come."[2] This generation is, perhaps, more familiar with the popular adaption:

> Christ has died.
> Christ has risen.
> Christ will come again.[3]

Indeed. So, are we awed?

God seems more interested in what we are becoming than in what we are giving up. As David sang,

> You do not delight in sacrifice, or I would bring it;
>   you do not take pleasure in burnt offerings.
> My sacrifice, O God, is a broken spirit;
>   a broken and contrite heart
>   you, God, will not despise. (Psalm 51:16–17)

Faith, in general, is less about the sacrifice of stuff and more about the surrender of our souls. Lent, in kind, is less about well-mannered denials and more about thinning our lives in order to thicken our communion with God.

Decrease is holy only when its destination is love.

Reflection

Reflect upon your personal preparation for Easter to date. Recall any knowledge of the church's historical Lenten practices. If this is not your first experience, in what ways have you thinned your life in order to thicken your communion with God in previous seasons?

Now consider a key question: why are you setting aside forty days to honor Jesus' death and resurrection this year?

Today's Fast: Lent As Project

Lent is often, and understandably, described with project language. The season has a starting date, an ending date, and clear, quantifiable goals "to accomplish" in between. After Easter, consequently, we evaluate Lent with project language. We "did okay" or "only made it two weeks" or "kept our commitment" or "totally failed."

Whether engaging this experience prior to Easter, or at another time during the year, from day one, I invite you to consider Lent as less of a project and more of a sojourn. A sojourn is a "temporary stay at a place."[4] And a "stay" is about presence, not productivity. For the next forty days, fast measuring your "success" statistically—that is, resist calculating how often you keep your commitment to do without meat or sugar or your favorite shows. Instead, invest your energy in seeking to remain present to the sacred history of Jesus' walk to the cross. With each reading, dust

> "Spiritual disciplines do not transform, they only become relational opportunities to open the heart to the Spirit who transforms."
> —JOHN H. COE[5]

off your childhood imagination and "stay" in each story. Observe Jesus' response to John's death. Imagine yourself as one of the disciples trying in vain to hush blind Bartimaeus. Throw your only cloak under the colt's hooves as Jesus enters Jerusalem. Taste the mounting tension as Jesus offends leaders with parables. Hear Jesus predict Peter's denial.

Fast Lent as project and enter Lent as experience, as a sojourn with your Savior.

On Lent

"What is your commitment this year, Mommy?" my daughter inquired with discerning eyes. The previous year, we both made commitments to honor the poor. Keona did what she loved and baked to raise funds for children in need. I devoted the entire year to simplicity, choosing to abstain from spending money on adding anything physical to my personal life—from shampoo to shoes. "This year I am fasting sugar and desserts," I replied. Then Keona offered one word that connected my then-ten-year-old with the wisest of ancient thinkers: "Why?"

Why, indeed.

My annual fasts, seasonal forty-day fasts, and weekly twelve- to twenty-four-hour fasts are more love offerings than disciplines, though it certainly requires discipline to maintain them. In short, I ache. I ache for my Bridegroom. I ache to live every waking moment conscious of His presence. I ache to live aware of His past and present suffering. I ache to live unattached to what man counts and measures. In many ways, all fasts are Lenten experiences, and as with the history of Lent, it is difficult for me to discern which came first: the discipline of fasting or the journey of Lent. Did they grow up together? Did one mature into the other? Are they two distinct experiences that fused over time? These are the questions that, in part, make the early origins of Lent difficult to discern.

For daily readings, I have chosen to offer small passages (beginning with Jesus' anointing at Bethany) from the gospel of John. Savor these sentences like a perfect cup of coffee or chunk of chocolate. Place yourself in the story and let the words melt in your mind. Then journal your reflections about the day.[6]

Today's Reading: John 12:1–11

_____

_____

_____

_____

_____

_____

_____

_____

_____

_____

_____

_____

_____

_____

DAY TWO

Christian spirituality, the contemplative life, is not about us.
It is about God. The great weakness of American spirituality
is that it is all about us: fulfilling our potential, getting the
blessings of God, expanding our influence, finding our gifts,
getting a handle on principles by which we can get an edge
over the competition. The more there is of us, the less there
is of God.

—EUGENE PETERSON[1]

Though uttered with reference to his (and my) culture, Eugene Peterson's insight has global relevance, for it reveals the church's spiritualization of an insatiable narcissism. Self cannot satisfy self, no matter how frequently it feasts. Lent is a much-needed mentor in an age obsessed with visible, measurable, manageable, and tweetable increase, for it invites us to walk with Jesus and His disciples through darker seasons that we would rather avoid: grief, conflict, misunderstanding, betrayal, restriction, rejection, and pain. Then Easter leads us in celebration of salvation as the stunningly satisfying fruit of Jesus' sacred decrease. A thoughtful Lenten journey directly confronts our modern obsession with increase and introduces us to unexpected friends of spiritual formation.

At least since the Council of Nicea in AD 325, Lent has been a forty-day, communal focus upon the most disillusioning season of the first disciples' lives. Jesus, having confessed to be the Messiah, prophesies His soon-coming death. Jesus, who commands winds and waves, allows Himself to be arrested. Jesus, who bests the brightest Pharisees and Sadducees, refuses to defend Himself when falsely accused. Jesus, who raised others from the dead, chooses not to save Himself.

> "A thought comes to me that troubles me and gives me no rest. It is not strong enough to make me act; it only hinders my progress toward virtue. A vigilant man would shake it off and arise for prayer."
>
> —ABBA THEODORE OF SCETIS (C. 4TH CENTURY)[2]

In Jesus' journey cross-ward, the disciples' illusions of what Jesus could and should do with His power were shattered by the reality of what Jesus actually did with His power, and their personal illusions of commitment-unto-death were shattered by the reality of fear-inspired self-protection. Meditating upon Jesus' suffering and the disciples' disillusionment creates a framework within which we can spiritually process our own loss of illusions and gaining of realities. This is critical, because in the words of Dr. Dan B. Allender and Dr. Tremper Longman III, "reality is where we meet God."[3] Therefore, as Jesuit Robert F. Taft eloquently said, through Lent let us:

> Enter into the desert of our hearts where, removed from side issues, we can face what we are, and in compunction, *penthos*, over that reality, let us ... [die] to self so that we may live for others, as we make vigil before the coming of the Lord.[4]

Reflection

French monk Bernard of Clairvaux (1090–1153) spoke of "four degrees of love" in his little book, *On the Love of God*: love of self for self's sake, love of God for self's sake, love of God for God's sake, and love of self for God's sake.[5] In light of Eugene Peterson's quote that began today's reading, ponder the difference between Clairvaux's first and fourth degrees of love.

Today's Fast: Regrets

Approaching a fresh endeavor can be both energizing and stressful. New is inspiring. New is enlightening. And new is, oddly enough, a reminder of what is now old. When fresh beginnings are stalked by the memories of stale endings, a sickly substance can steal our strength: regret. Regret empties anticipation, flattens dreams, and suffocates hope, because regret is a form of self-punishment. Whereas hindsight helps us learn from the past, regret beats us up with the past.

So for one entire day (or go for forty), I invite you to fast regret. Do not feed it. Do not give it space. Let it go: God's mercies are "new every morning" (Lamentations 3:23). And meditate on Jesus' glorious promise from Revelation 21:5: "I am making everything new!"

On Lent

Before us lies a two-thousand-year-old heirloom quilt. Some portions are missing. They have slipped into the dark chasm of lost history, leaving nothing but space and speculation. Other portions are obviously unoriginal. They bear the loving evidence of a repatching, a rezoning, an offering of newer fabric sewn by less ancient hands.

Much work has been done by many scholars to reconstruct what is now absent, to track the origin of what remains, to trace the source of each worn, faith-sewn thread back to its beginnings. However, beginnings are mysterious things: part breath, part hope, part fumble, part grace. Roots are, historically, perhaps the most humble of God's creations on earth. They require neither acknowledgment nor praise. Their reward is reaped when the living stand upon them and reach for the fruit the roots made possible. Such is the story of Lent. The weighty beauty of this heirloom rests not in its satisfyingly discernible beginning, but in the warmth of soul it still offers to communities and individuals today.

Today's Reading: John 12:12–19

_____

_____

_____

_____

_____

_____

_____

_____

_____

DAY THREE

He must become greater; I must become less.

—JOHN 3:30

Decrease is a spiritual necessity. John the Baptist was the first among Jesus' followers to grasp its countercultural power. "Less is more" is a popular simplicity mantra in our day. But John's understanding of "less is more" was spiritually profound. Gabriel had announced John's life-calling to Zechariah before John was even conceived: John was the one who, "in the spirit and power of Elijah . . . [would] make ready a people prepared for the Lord" (Luke 1:17). In many ways, John lived a Lenten lifestyle 365 days a year. His diet was narrow, his possessions were minimal, and his focus was eternal. But decrease for John was less about assets and more about attention. His longing was to draw his generation's attention and allegiance to the

> "[The dark night of the soul] strengthens and purifies the love that is of God, and takes away and destroys the other."
>
> —JOHN OF THE CROSS (1542–1591)[1]

11

Messiah. From John's perspective, the true value of people seeing him was that people would then be positioned to see through him and gaze at Jesus. By willingly decreasing, John increased others' view of the Savior.

Attention is not innately evil. It becomes evil when used as a self-serving end instead of a God-serving means. Those who steward attention as means and not end stand tall and serve strong, knowing that all gifts come from God and can therefore draw attention to God. Praise slides off such souls like water off a window[2] into a cup that is offered to God alone. Surrounded by swelling crowds, John directed his fans to Jesus.

> The next day John saw Jesus coming toward him and said, "Look, the Lamb of God, who takes away the sin of the world! This is the one I meant when I said, 'A man who comes after me has surpassed me because he was before me.' I myself did not know him, but the reason I came baptizing with water was that he might be revealed to Israel." (John 1:29–31)

John decreased so others could see the Lamb. John decreased so others could follow the One who preceded and surpassed him (John 1:30). John decreased so that the Messiah would be revealed in John's lifetime. May our decrease likewise increase our generation's view of Jesus.

Reflection

In his day, a psalmist sang: "Not to us, LORD, not to us but to your name be the glory, because of your love and faithfulness" (Psalm 115:1). Think of models in your lifetime of individuals who—like the psalmist in the Old Testament and John the Baptist in the New Testament—used the attention they received to increase others' view of God. Then reflect on ways that you are following (or in the future can follow) their example.

Today's Fast: Collecting Praise

Biographer Carole C. Carlson said of Corrie Ten Boom:

> Her remarkable ministry became known to millions through both the book and movie version of *The Hiding Place*. She never looked at fame as being the culmination of personal triumph. To Corrie it was simply a result of God's plans. Her way of handling adulation was to take each compliment as a flower, and then gather them all in a bouquet and give them back to Jesus by saying, "Here Lord, they belong to You."[3]

Make an effort today to follow Corrie's example and fast collecting praise. The key to this fast is redirection, not deflection. Whereas deflection discounts and rejects praise, redirection stewards and then deposits praise at the feet of the One to whom it is due. Sincerely receive any affirmation today without apology and then tonight, offer Jesus a bouquet of praise. If at day's end you find your intended bouquet sparse, fill it in with gratitude for God's work in your life.

On Lent

The etymology of the word *Lent* enjoys an easy consensus among scholars. In earlier times, the English word *Lent* carried the meaning of "springtime." As *The Lenten Triodion* poetically states, "Lent signifies not winter but spring, not darkness but light, not death but renewed vitality."[4] According to Fr. William P. Saunders, professor of catechetics and theology at Christendom's Notre Dame Graduate School in Alexandria, the Anglo-Saxon word *lectentid* "literally means not only 'springtide' but also was the word for 'March,' the month in which the majority of Lent falls."[5] In Greek, *Lent* is *tessarakosti*, and in Latin, *quadragesima*, both of which emphasize the number forty, a number rich in biblical significance.

In origin, however, Lent's history is far less obvious. Fifty years ago, the history of Lent could have been penned with greater certainty . . . and with greater error. Scholars affirm that we simply know less than we used to about Lent. Catholic scholar Nicholas V. Russo explains that, "today the history of Lent's origins is far less certain because many of the suppositions upon which the standard theory rested have been cast into doubt."[6]

Today's Reading: John 12:20–28

_____

_____

_____

_____

_____

_____

_____

_____

_____

DAY FOUR

Whereas decreasing in attention is evident at the beginning of John's public ministry, decreasing in confidence is evident toward the end. The latter is infinitely more trying than the former. When mumblers came to John asking how he could have possibly overlooked requiring the new guy to sign a non-compete clause, John's Jordan River proclamation was a manifesto:

> The bride belongs to the bridegroom. The friend who attends the bridegroom waits and listens for him, and is full of joy when he hears the bridegroom's voice. That joy is mine, and it is now complete. (John 3:29)

John refused to compete with Jesus. Instead of collecting attention, John directed attention back to the Bridegroom. We heard no hesitation in John's voice from the Jordan: Jesus was the One he had been waiting for. However, a year later John's voice from prison sounded less certain. Surrounded by paid guards instead of volunteer crowds, John sent his disciples to ask Jesus, "Are you the one who was to come, or should we expect someone else?" (Matthew 11:3).

Only Jesus and John know what fully prompted John's question. But perhaps Jesus' response offers us a glimpse into the source of John's uncertainty. After reminding John (via the witness of John's disciples) of His ministry of healing and hope, Jesus said, "Blessed is anyone who does not stumble on account of me" (Matthew 11:6). Initially, this statement seems oddly out of place following a mention of Messiah-endorsing miracles. Yet somehow Jesus' actions were not matching John's expectations. And that distance between what John thought Jesus would do and what Jesus actually did was straining John's certainty of who Jesus was. In this sense, Lent came early for John. He experienced from prison what the first disciples later would experience throughout Jesus' Passion, and what we still ponder two millennia later.

> "God needs nothing, asks nothing, and demands nothing, like the stars. It is life with God which demands these things. . . . You do not have to sit outside in the dark. If, however, you want to look at the stars, you will find that the darkness is necessary. But the stars neither require nor demand it."
>
> —ANNIE DILLARD[1]

Jesus' ways are often unexpected. Jesus' words can seem oddly out of place. From within prisons of pain or persecution, injustice or accusation, limitations or unmet longings, we, too, can wonder if Jesus is truly who we thought He was. A key invitation of our spiritual journeys is to be emotionally honest about our uncertainties. Questions such as the one asked by John are signs of a living, growing, active faith, not evidence of a dying one. Jesus' calm response to John echoes to us today: "Recall what I have done in the past. Accept me as the Great I Am of your future."

Reflection

Has the distance between what you thought Jesus would do and what Jesus actually did ever caused tremors of uncertainty in your soul? How did you respond to the uncertainty? Today, follow John's example: ask Jesus frank questions, and then wait for His response.

Today's Fast: Artificial Light

In the Eastern Orthodox tradition, there is a moving moment on Cheese-fare Sunday[2] in which all lights in the church are extinguished. In the subsequent darkness, the community begins to "wander forty days through the desert of Lent."[3] Picture John the Baptist in prison. Imagine what he might have seen, heard, and felt. Then unplug from the power grid and read Hebrews 11 aloud by candlelight.

On Lent

Several ancient pre-Nicene texts are consistently referenced by Catholic, Orthodox, and Protestant scholars alike in the search for the origins of Lent. In Table 1, I have attempted to list and organize these texts by approximate dates and key phrases.

TABLE 1. PRE-NICENE TEXTS REFERENCED IN
SCHOLARSHIP REGARDING THE ORIGIN OF LENT

In between the "one day," "two days," or "forty hours" seen in the *Apostolic Tradition*,[6] Tertullian,[7] and Irenaeus and the "forty days" of *Canon 1 of St. Peter*,[8] *Canons of Hippolytus*,[9] and Origen,[10] Dionysius of Alexandria[11] and the *Didascalia Apostolorum* refer to a six-day "fast in the days of Pascha from the second day of the week."[12] At first glance, then, ancient pre-Nicene texts speak of a one- to two-day, or forty-hour, fast immediately preceding Resurrection Sunday; a six-day pre-paschal fast; and fasts of forty days.

APPROXIMATE DATES	ANCIENT WORK OR AUTHOR	KEY CONCEPTS AND PHRASES
c. 120–c. 202	St. Irenaeus of Lyons (Gaul)	fast, variety, one day or two, forty hours
c. 150–c. 212	Tertullian (North Africa), *Concerning Baptism* 19; *On the Fasts* 2, 13–14 (*Patrologia Latina*) ii, 956, 971–974.	one day, forty hours
2nd C	Didache	fast, baptism, preparation for the sacrament[4]
2nd C	Justin Martyr in First Apology, 61	fasting, baptismal candidates[5]
c. 185–c. 254	Origen, *Homilies on Leviticus* 10.2:5–6	forty days, fasting
c. 215 (if authored by Hippolytus)	*Apostolic Tradition* 2, 30, 2–9; 21, 1–5	final examination and preparation in the days before Baptism (ch. 20), fasting (ch. 23), fasting at Easter (ch. 33)
50 years after Origen?	*Canons of Hippolytus*	fast, the forty, God fasted on our behalf
d. 264	Dionysius of Alexandria	fast of up to six days
c. 313	*Canon 1 of St. Peter of Alexandria*	other forty days, bewailing their faults
3rd C	*Didascalia Apostolorum*	fast, days of Pascha, from the second day of the week

Today's Reading: John 12:29–36

_____

_____

_____

_____

_____

_____

_____

_____

_____

_____

_____

_____

_____

_____

DAY FIVE

Jesus' response assured John of more than Jesus' identity. Jesus' words affirmed John's identity as well. Returning to their mentor, John's disciples testified, "The blind receive sight, the lame walk, those who have leprosy are cleansed, the deaf hear, the dead are raised, and the good news is proclaimed to the poor" (Matthew 11:5). In other words, Isaiah 61 was being fulfilled. The Spirit of the Lord was upon Jesus. Jesus was who John thought He was: the Messiah. Which meant, conversely, that John was who God said he was: the prophet sent to prepare the way for the Lord.[1] Such a calling is understandably easier to believe by the waters of the Jordan than from within the walls of a prison.

Perhaps that is, in part, what can make questioning so painful. For the faithful Christ-follower, self-concept is inextricably connected to God-concept. We are valuable because God is Creator. We are forgiven because God is Redeemer. If God is not who we thought He was, then who are we? Many of us dare not even ask the question. Do we fear that God will fail the test? Dr. Leonard Sweet teaches that in the Jewish culture,

> It's an act of reverence to ask questions of the story. The Jews are confident that the story is strong enough to be tried and tested....Around

21

the table, a Jewish child has "That's a good question!" drummed into his or her soul, not, "You don't ask that question"... Questions are as sacred as answers.[2]

We weaken—not strengthen—our faith when we silence sincere questions. Faith in Christ is not an airy substance that rests on unquestioning souls. Biblical faith is muscular, thickened more through trials than ease. The Author of our faith is more than able to address the identity crises His unexpected words and ways may trigger.

John heard within Jesus' response the same striking answer that we hear today: Who is Jesus? Jesus is more than we thought, hoped, or imagined. His wildness is a source of wonder, not of worry. His righteousness is deeper than the oceans. His goodness is higher than the heavens.

> "We are not necessarily doubting that God will do the best for us; we are wondering how painful the best will turn out to be."
> —C. S. Lewis (1898–1963)[3]

His faithfulness exceeds our comprehension. So what does that make us? Loved. Who are we? Christ's beloved. We are loved when making bold proclamations near cool waters under sunny skies. We are loved when asking sincere questions in dark cells and darker times. We are loved.

Reflection

Jesus described John as "more than a prophet" and the greatest man "born of women" after—not before—John posed his please-confirm-your-identity interrogative (Matthew 11:9, 11). John's question did not make Jesus nervous. Reflect on the questions patriarchs, prophets, and kings have asked God throughout the ages, such as Jeremiah's respectful questioning of God's justice below:

You are always righteous, LORD,
>   when I bring a case before you.
Yet I would speak with you about your justice:
>   Why does the way of the wicked prosper?
>   Why do all the faithless live at ease? (Jeremiah 12:1)

Today's Fast: Tidy Faith

If we view faith and doubt as antonyms, we will be tempted to interpret John's question as something other than spiritual uncertainty. Perhaps, we may reason, John was confident but wanted his disciples to hear about the miracles from the Source, or perhaps John sent his disciples with the hope that they would start following Jesus themselves, or . . .

Or perhaps John had doubts. Theologian Peter Abelard (1079–1142) stated, "By doubting we come to inquiry, by inquiry we come to truth."[4] Today let your faith be messy. Fast tidying it up to make it more tame, and meditate upon Jesus' peaceful (and even affirming) response to John's uncertainty.

On Lent

Irenaeus was mentored by Polycarp who sat at the feet of the apostle John. His words, which come to us through Eusebius's chronicles of church history, have understandably been cited repeatedly on the subject of Lent's ancient origins:

> The dispute is not only about the day, but also about the actual character of the fast. Some think that they ought to fast for one day, some for two, others for still more; some make their "day" last forty hours on end.[5]

Upon reading the surrounding text in Eusebius's *History of the Church*, it appears that from Eusebius's perspective—writing over a hundred years after Irenaeus's death—"the dispute" referred to a serious disagreement between churches in Asia and the church in Rome over when "the paschal fast"[6] should end. An assembly of bishops ruled in favor of what Eusebius described as, "the practice which, *from apostolic tradition*, has prevailed to the present time, of terminating the fast on no other day than on that of the resurrection of our Saviour."[7]

Today's Reading: John 12:37–43

_____

_____

_____

_____

_____

_____

_____

_____

_____

_____

DAY SIX

Fifteen months[1] after John the Baptist was imprisoned, Herod Antipas—the son of Herod the Great who reigned at the time of Jesus' birth—beheaded John to save face at a banquet.[2] John's decrease was now complete. All eyes turned to Jesus. Matthew recorded that, "When Jesus heard what had happened, he withdrew by boat privately to a solitary place" (Matthew 14:13). In the manna-for-multitudes and gravity-defying miracles that follow, it is easy for us to overlook and underestimate Jesus' grief. But after Jesus healed and fed the thousands who awaited Him in the no-longer-solitary place and before Jesus and Peter walked on water in a storm,

> Jesus made the disciples get into the boat and go on ahead of him to the other side, while he dismissed the crowd. After he had dismissed them, he went up on a mountainside by himself to pray. Later that night, he was there alone. (Matthew 14:22–23)

At this point in Jesus' life, few remained alive of those who had witnessed His angel-celebrated birth and grasped at least in part the

> "We have never reaped such a harvest from any seed as from that which fell from our hands while tears were falling from our eyes."
>
> —C. H. SPURGEON (1834–1892)[3]

heavenly weight of His messianic anointing. Zechariah and Elizabeth, righteous Simeon and the prophetess Anna, the Magi, the shepherds, and probably even Joseph had died. The crowds were curious as well as clueless. The disciples were devoted as long as there was little danger. But John knew who Jesus was. John attested to Jesus' divine Son-ship when he leaped in Elizabeth's womb at the sound of Mary's greeting, when he baptized Jesus and heard God's voice through the open heavens at the Jordan, and when he asked Jesus to confirm His identity from within the prison that would be John's last home on earth.

> "[God] draws the curtain about the bed of his chosen sufferer and, at the same time, he withdraws another curtain which before concealed his Glory!"
>
> —C. H. SPURGEON (1834–1892)[5]

Now, John was gone and Jesus needed solitude to pray. John's death marks a turn toward the cross in Jesus' ministry. From this point forward, Jesus more intensely taught upon and demonstrated the revolutionary nature of His "upside down" kingdom.[4] Consequently, the religious tension that eventually nailed him to the cross dramatically escalated. Alone on that mountain, as Jesus grieved John's death, He anticipated His own.

Reflection

Bring to mind the names and faces of loved ones who have died. What deposits did they make in your life? How did you feel when you first learned of their deaths? Allow your experiences to infuse feeling into the written account of Jesus' prayerful mourning on the mountainside.

Today's Fast: Speeding Past Sorrow

Jesus sets an example for us all to sit with our sorrow. He could have easily kept moving in an attempt to distance Himself from sadness. Instead, Jesus sent everyone away and carved out space to pray in solitude. Deaths are defining moments in our lives. It serves us poorly to hurry past them. Today, honor the losses in your life. Instead of speeding past sadness, slow down and be present to your emotions. With Jesus, sit with your sorrow and let loss do its eternal work in your soul.

On Lent

After the assembly's ruling, Bishop Polycrates wrote a letter defending the Asian church's continued observance of ending the fast at Passover, based upon the practices of many "great lights"[6] who had served and died in Asia.[7] In context, Irenaeus's oft-quoted words were written as a response to an escalation in this conflict. His letter was penned to rebuke and correct the actions of Victor I, Bishop of Rome, who dramatically excommunicated the churches of Asia in response to Polycrates's letter. To what extent Victor's reaction had to do with exerting the supremacy of the Church of Rome, movements away from traditional Jewish customs, or the actual practice of fasting, we are left to wonder. However, Irenaeus's words of correction are clarion: his concern was peace, not practice.

Today's Reading: John 12:44–50

_____

_____

_____

_____

_____

_____

_____

_____

_____

_____

_____

_____

_____

_____

_____

DAY SEVEN

Rising from prayer, Jesus descended the mountainside and walked on water toward His storm-tormented disciples. Fear, by nature, distorts reality. Terrified, the disciples mistook Jesus for a ghost. We know the story well. Eyewitnesses Matthew and John affirm that as soon as Jesus stepped into the boat, the storm subsided and the boat reached the shore.[1] The miracles prompted a revelation. Still in the boat, the disciples worshipped Jesus, confessing, "Truly you are the Son of God" (Matthew 14:33). Shortly afterward, Peter exclaimed, "You are the Messiah, the Son of the living God" (Matthew 16:16). In each synoptic Gospel,[2] Peter's proclamation is followed by Jesus' first prediction of His coming death:

> The Son of Man must suffer many things and be rejected by the elders, the chief priests and the teachers of the law, and he must be killed and on the third day be raised to life. (Luke 9:21–22)

Revelations are often followed by trials. Perhaps they are preparation for them. Still, this was unexpected: manna for multitudes, water-walking, silencing storms and . . . death? No wonder Peter rebuked Jesus! But wait, there is more:

Whoever wants to be my disciple, must deny themselves and take up their cross daily and follow me. For whoever wants to save their life, will lose it, but whoever loses their life for me will save it. (Luke 9:23–24)

It is probably impossible for us to comprehend—in a culture of dazzling, diamond-studded crosses—what images Jesus' words projected into the minds of the disciples. In Jesus' day, crucifixion was considered to be the cruelest possible form of punishment.[4] Without question, *Take Up Your Cross and Die* was not the slogan the Twelve were hoping to champion when they became Jesus' followers. In that regard, precious little has changed.

> "To endure the cross is not tragedy; it is the suffering which is the fruit of an exclusive allegiance to Jesus Christ. When it comes, it is not an accident, but a necessity."
>
> —DIETRICH BONHOEFFER
> (1906–1945)[3]

Reflection

As you read Leonard Sweet's quote below, reflect upon what taking up your cross means to you today.

On the cross, leadership dies. On the cross, success dies. On the cross, skills die, and excellence dies. All of my strengths—nailed to the cross. All of my weaknesses—nailed to the cross. All of my yearnings for bigger and better, for anything other than Christ himself—nailed to that same cross.[5]

Today's Fast: A Meal

In a world where people are afraid to fast because it may seem too difficult, inconvenient, and burdensome, the Church reminds us of the meaning of fasting: to hunger and tire to the point of physical exhaustion for the sake of uniting with our heavenly Bridegroom.

—JOHN PAUL ABDELSAYED[6]

Earlier, John's disciples had asked why Jesus' disciples did not observe the customary fasts. Jesus replied, "How can the guests of the bridegroom mourn while he is with them? The time will come when the bridegroom will be taken from them; then they will fast" (Matthew 9:15). In His response, Jesus associated fasting with mourning. Though there are numerous motivations and methods of fasting, today I invite you to experience what some refer to as a Bridegroom Fast[7] as we reflect on the first time Jesus told His disciples of His soon-coming death. In this type of fast, the ache to eat an earthly meal serves to kindle an ache to partake of what the apostle John called the "wedding supper of the Lamb" (Revelation 19:9). During the time you would have been eating, read Revelation 22:1–16, and then slowly read verse 17 multiple times.

On Lent

Of interest is the difference in tone between Irenaeus's actual words below and the historical context supplied by Eusebius:

And this variety in its observance has not originated in our time; but long before in that of our ancestors. It is likely that they did not hold to strict accuracy, and thus formed a custom for their posterity according to their own simplicity and peculiar mode. Yet all of these lived none the less in peace, and we also live in peace with one another; and the disagreement in regard to the fast confirms the agreement in the faith.[8]

Irenaeus, writing closer to the day of the apostles, emphasized a long history of living in peace with varied fasting practices. Eusebius, writing closer to the day of unprecedented favor for Christians, identified two "customs," and grants one the status of "apostolic tradition." Perhaps focus on manifest customs flourishes in times of favor. Or, conversely, perhaps focus on faith-fueled unity flourishes in times when the church is regularly reminded that they are aliens and strangers on this earth.

Today's Reading: John 13:1–7

_____

_____

_____

_____

_____

_____

_____

_____

_____

_____

DAY EIGHT

I wonder if Peter rebuked Jesus as the spokesman for all the Twelve. Surely, Jesus' talk of crosses and death would have been deeply unsettling for His followers, especially in light of the miracles they had witnessed. Approaching their two-year mark as Jesus' inner circle, the disciples had seen a dead girl come back to life, a demon-possessed man returned to peaceful sanity, storms calmed, bodies healed, bread multiplied, and, most recently, the Messiah walk on water.

Miracles, evidently, had not adequately prepared them to welcome crucifixion. The problem, of course, is not with the miracles themselves but rather with our perception of the miracles. We tend to view a miracle as a divine deposit on more miracles. We like our miracles to be perpetual, thank you. Once raised, we want Lazarus to live forever. But he cannot. So we are bewildered when the recipient of the miracle still dies. It seems to me that miracles are less of a promise for tomorrow and more of a manifestation of God's love and power for today. Today, God provides bread. Today, God calms the storm. Tomorrow's needs and storms cannot void the reality of today's miracles any more than today's miracles can void the potential of tomorrow's needs and storms.

I, too, have been bewildered by miracles big and small. With the latter, I have watched "only-God" miracle writing opportunities produce beautiful books that collected dust in forgotten warehouses. With the former, I have accompanied friends whose "only-God" miracle pregnancies ended in miscarriage. The church in general panics when miracles miscarry. We scurry clumsily about to prop up God's sagging reputation. *There must have been a problem,* we offer. *God must have something even better around the corner,* we propose. Must He? Here, then is my Lenten plea for the day: let the mourning mourn. Grant those who grieve the dignity to ask questions. Bestow upon the bewildered permission to not edit their honesty.

Crucifixion is, after all, serious work.

> "I do not want to fix myself. I cannot fix myself. My natural fortitude served me well as a young believer and it was inevitable that I was habituated from birth to live in the power of self. But as I grow older in the faith, I find that I am invited by the Spirit to learn to give up the project of moralism, of trying to fix myself by my spiritual efforts. Rather, I want to open more deeply to Christ's work on the cross and the work of the Spirit in my deep for my daily bread."
>
> —JOHN H. COE[1]

Reflection

Recall miracles that ended in heartbreak: the faith venture that went bankrupt, the pregnancy that miscarried, the new job with the difficult boss. When, if ever, have you felt the need to "prop up God's sagging reputation"?

Today's Fast: Fixing It

Six years before I met my husband, his first wife died in a tragic car accident. The two loved God and one another and were headed back to seminary from celebrating Christmas with their families when they hit an ice-covered stretch of road. Barry explained that following the accident the greatest gift people gave him was their supportive presence. The most hurtful offerings came from those who tried to fix Barry's pain with platitudes such as *God picks His favorite flowers for His heavenly garden*. Or *You're young; you will remarry*. Such clumsy attempts to fix someone else's pain reflect the probability that we are uncomfortable facing our own. So today, fast fixing things. Let the broken be broken for a day—be that a tool or a heart.

On Lent

Fr. William P. Saunders asserts that, "Lent became more regularized after the legalization of Christianity in AD 313."[2] Late nineteenth-century Anglican minister Herman Lilienthal Lonsdale agrees, theorizing that the "tendency of thought within the Church now led to centralization and some seat of authority. The influence of the State upon the Church became paramount, and it looked to the State for models of its constitutions, division, usages."[3] Or as Dr. Leah Payne suggests, "As the Church grew, it needed uniformity in practice to keep uniformity in orthodoxy."[4] By motivations that, no doubt, ranged from the pursuit of doctrinal purity to the pursuit of positional power, a historic council in AD 325 profoundly affected Lent as it is experienced and honored today.

Today's Reading: John 13:8–17

_____

_____

_____

_____

_____

_____

_____

_____

_____

_____

_____

_____

_____

DAY NINE

Any hope the disciples may have had for Jesus' curious cross-talk to fade as He gained distance from His cousin's cruel demise was short-lived. Now that they knew who He was—the Son of God, the Christ—Jesus regularly reminded them where He was going. Throughout the subsequent year, Jesus spoke often and openly about the cost of following Christ crossward into His upside-down kingdom. His illustrations were startling: good Samaritans, Nineveh judging future generations, the first being last, narrow doors, great banquets given away to strangers, lost sheep, a found son, rich men in hell, and poor men in heaven. And then, days before Jesus' triumphal entry into Jerusalem, He once again made His path as plain as possible:

> Jesus took the Twelve aside and told them, "We are going up to Jerusalem, and everything that is written by the prophets about the Son of Man will be fulfilled. He will be delivered to the Gentiles. They will mock him, insult him and spit on him; they will flog him and kill him. On the third day he will rise again."
>
> The disciples did not understand any of this. Its meaning was hidden from them, and they did not know what he was talking about. (Luke 18:31–34)

Why does Jesus speak words that He knows we cannot understand? Would it not be more logical for God to conserve His voice—that is, be silent—when our comprehension is frail and offer His voice—that is, with amplified explanations—when our comprehension is strong? Welcome, once again, to the surprising kingdom of God. Though I can only guess about God's motives, I do know mine: as a parent I speak as an investment in my children's futures, even when they cannot understand. My eldest has often said sincerely, "I'm sorry, Mom. I know what you're saying is important. But all I hear is 'blah, blah, blah.'" "It's okay," I reply. "I know you're trying. So I'll write down what I'm saying for you in case you need it in the future." Jonathan posts my words on his walls and tapes my illustrations to his closet doors. And when, on occasion, I have offered to take them down, he replies, "No, Mom. I still need them."

> "No matter how we rationalize, God will sometimes seem unfair from the perspective of a person trapped in time. . . . Not until history has run its course will we understand how 'all things work together for good.' Faith means believing in advance what will only make sense in reverse."
>
> —PHILIP YANCEY[1]

Be they plain or shrouded in mystery, God's words are infinitely more needful. So let us post them on our minds and hide them in our hearts. Let us honor God's words and be encouraged: our lack of understanding cannot sabotage the power or the purpose of His voice.

Reflection

Thankfully, human reasoning neither leads nor limits God's love. Consider passages in Scripture in which God's words escape your understanding. What would it be like if God withheld His voice until humankind could fully comprehend it?

Today's Fast: Rationalism

This may be impossible, but today we are going to attempt to fast the belief that reason is king. Rationalism, a child of the Enlightenment, is the "practice of treating reason as the ultimate authority in religion."[2] Robert K. Merton explains that the early champions of rationalism were men of deep faith who,

> Laud[ed] the faculty of reason. . . . Reason is praiseworthy because man, chosen of God, alone possesses it; it serves to differentiate him from the beasts of the field . . . it possesses still another exemplary characteristic; it enables man more fully to glorify God by aiding him to appreciate His works. . . . Hence, it becomes imperative for them who would rationalize these doctrines to "prove" that reason and faith—two such highly exalted virtues of the Puritan—are not inconsistent.[3]

However, it is not possible to prove with the mind what is born of the spirit. Early Puritan scientists reduced nature to matter and, as Peter Homans succinctly summarizes, "rationalized and disenchanted the biblical Christian world of spirit."[4]

Which brings us to a day in which believing anything that cannot be reproduced and verified in a laboratory is considered a "leap of faith." No. It is just faith—the same faith that gave reason wings. Respectful consideration of the deep intimacy with God experienced by some whose faculties of reason are considered "impaired" should inspire humility of mind within us. As you consider today to what extent reason is king to you, reflect upon the following two quotes from anthropologist Paul Stoller and King Solomon:

> No matter the logical consistency of our propositions and semi-propositions, no matter how deeply we think we have mastered a subject, the world, for the embodied scholar, remains a wondrous

place that stirs the imagination and sparks creativity. Those who struggle with humility, no matter their scholarly station, admit willingly that they have much to learn from forgetful old men and women who, at first glance, seem to have little knowledge to impart.[5]

Trust in the LORD with all of your heart
And lean not on your own understanding;
In all your ways submit to him,
And he will make your paths straight. (Proverbs 3:5–6)

On Lent

For two months in AD 325, bishops convened for the First Council of Nicea, which was convoked by Constantine. Christology was the critical discussion of the hour, and amidst the prayerful days and months, a decision was made that set a cornerstone for the development of Lent. As Dr. Nicholas V. Russo of the University of Notre Dame explains,

The Council of Nicea issued canons intended to bring general alignment on matters of liturgical practice and church organization. Among these was the establishment of a common date for the Easter feast that, up until that time, had been commemorated on different days in a given year depending on the method of calculation.[6]

We can surmise that Lent's establishment before Easter was part of a broader movement toward alignment and standardization begun at the Council of Nicea and continued throughout the fourth century.[7]

Only following the Council of Nicea in AD 325 did the length of Lent become fixed at forty days, and then only nominally.[8]

Today's Reading: John 13:18–30

_____

_____

_____

_____

_____

_____

_____

_____

_____

_____

_____

_____

_____

_____

DAY TEN

Following Jesus' most recent reminder of His coming death, Matthew and Mark recorded a story about the sons of Zebedee that has often been explained as a bold, but naïve, attempt to secure leadership spots in Jesus' coming kingdom. However, since Gospel writers sequenced stories with intentionality, I wonder if, in context, the brothers' request was motivated in part by a search for some semblance of control. With a perspective reminiscent of a cosmic game of musical chairs, John and James called dibs on the spots to the right and left of Jesus during His messianic reign. While Matthew stated that the brothers' mom championed the maneuvering, Mark laid responsibility for the religious positioning squarely upon the shoulders of John and James. Approaching Jesus, the sons of Zebedee requested a "favor." With a question He would—not coincidentally—soon pose verbatim to a blind beggar,[1] Jesus replied, "What do you want me to do for you?" (Mark 10:36). The two then said, "Let one of us sit at your right and the other at your left in your glory" (Mark 10:37).

Uncertainty is quite revealing. The unknown triggers different reactions in different hearts and exposes our souls' defaults. Ambiguity reveals where we instinctively go to feel the illusion of security again. In response to a yet-unnamed but imminent storm, some hide, some run, some live in denial, some escape into fictional worlds, some feast, and some stake out their territory. The latter we see in John and James's response to Jesus' continued cross-talk. All the uncertainty triggered something deep within the brothers. As they wrestled with the seemingly mixed messages of *Jesus as Messiah* and *Jesus crucified*, they reasoned it was time to take control.

What does uncertainty trigger within us? What defaults do we gravitate toward when facing the unknown? As the example of John and James clearly demonstrates, defaults—by and large—are self-serving. They take but do not give to those around us. Matthew records, "When the ten heard about this, they were indignant with the two brothers" (Matthew 20:24).

To change our defaults we must first address our theology of uncertainty. And to address our theology of uncertainty, we must first befriend mystery. Anglican clergyman Jeremy Taylor is quoted as saying, "[A] religion without mystery must be a religion without God."[2] Mystery is a given for relationship between the Infinite and the finite. As we follow Jesus into uncertainty, we are free, in the words of Gerald G. May, to "join the dance of life in fullness without having a clue about what the steps are."[3]

> "When we were children most of us were good friends with mystery. The world was full of it and we loved it. Then as we grew older we slowly accepted the indoctrination that mystery exists only to be solved. For many of us, mystery became an adversary; unknowing became a weakness. The contemplative spiritual life is an ongoing reversal of this adjustment. It is a slow and sometimes painful process of becoming 'as little children' again, in which we first make friends with mystery and finally fall in love again with it."
>
> —GERALD G. MAY[4]

Reflection

To dance when we do not know the steps requires us to value our Partner above our performance. To dance in the dark demonstrates a lavish display of trust. Lent, in its mystery, is an invitation to dance. In what areas of your life do you sense God's invitation to embrace mystery?

Today's Fast: Avoidance

Today, pay attention to avoidance mechanisms that surface when you face the unknown, unknowable, uncomfortable, or unavoidable. Do you eat more? Sleep more? Domineer more? Disappear more? Why? Ask God's Holy Spirit to sensitize you today to the existence of avoidance defaults in your life. Prayerfully consider what beliefs might underlie any avoidance that emerges when you are facing uncertainty. Return to John the Baptist's words, "He must increase, but I must decrease" (John 3:30 NASB), and consider what relevance John's wisdom might have as a guide through the unknown.

On Lent

In Day Eleven and Day Twelve, I will share Table 2, within which I have sought to compile the post-Nicene writings that reference the continuing development of Lent. When considered side by side, Tables 1 and 2 visually hint at the development of both fasting and pre-paschal practices in the fourth- and fifth-century church. References to one-day, two-day, and forty-hour fasts fade, and references to forty-day fasts become clearly prominent. The six-day fast, spoken of by Dionysius of Alexandria and in the *Didascalia Apostolorum*, seems to develop into (or be renamed as) a pre-paschal Holy Week (or Great

Week) fast.[5] Further, the post-Nicene forty-day fast references are distinctly associated with Pascha and/or baptism and/or penance. Please note that in Table 2, original document text is identified with quotations and the works that reference the original texts can be found in the Notes section.

Today's Reading: John 13:31–36

_____

_____

_____

_____

_____

_____

_____

_____

_____

_____

_____

DAY ELEVEN

With the toxic fumes of religious positioning lingering in their minds, Jesus' puzzled disciples packed their few belongings and continued traveling toward Jerusalem via Jericho and Bethany. Last steps and last stops are weighty indeed. What we do with our final breaths reflects the values we hold dear in life. So I find myself fascinated by what Jesus did and said between Jericho and Jerusalem.

Luke, as both doctor and historian, focused upon Jesus' interaction with two lives in that telling space: a blind beggar (whom Mark identified as Bartimaeus) and a wealthy tax collector named Zacchaeus. Both were at the bottom of the culture's class system. Both desperately wanted to see Jesus. In response, Jesus invested in them some of the final hours of what would be His final days. We know nothing of their backstories. But then, in many ways, backstories matter little once Jesus enters the room. As it did for these two men, whatever the cause of our physical and spiritual blindness, whatever family we do or do not have, whatever sins or successes we count as our own, Jesus' presence makes *this moment* the most important moment of our lives.

This moment for the blind beggar occurred on a dusty, dirty road-side. Hearing that Jesus was passing by, Bartimaeus ignored everyone's attempts to coach him or, perchance, intimidate him into a respectful silence. Instead he shouted, "Jesus, Son of David, have mercy on me!" (Luke 18:38). Luke records that Jesus heard the shout and had the beggar brought "near." How beautiful. *Near* is the fruit of perseverance, not passivity. Evidently, beggars can be choosers. This beggar chose Jesus. And now, Bartimaeus was also asked by Jesus to choose his heart's dearest request: "Lord, I want to see" (Luke 18:41). So see he did! What he *did not do* with his sight is notable. He did not return to the roadside to grab his stuff. He did not rush to the temple to have his stigma removed. He did not run ahead alone into the city and draw attention to himself. Bartimaeus used his sight to follow, praise, and draw attention to Jesus. In this, he demonstrated for centuries to come the way followers multiply miracles.

> "While fasting with the body, brethren, let us also fast in spirit. Let us loose every bond of iniquity; let us undo the knots of every contract made by violence; let us tear up all unjust agreements; let us give bread to the hungry and welcome to our house the poor who have no roof to cover them, that we may receive great mercy from Christ our God."
>
> —*THE LENTEN TRIODION*[1]

Reflection

As mentioned previously, the Gospel writers sequenced their stories with intentionality. Consider Luke's ordering of the surrounding text:

» Jesus tells the Parable of the Persistent Widow, who cried out for justice until she received it (Luke 18:1–8).

» Jesus tells the Parable of the Pharisee and the Tax Collector, in which the tax collector is described as justified before God (Luke 18:9–14).

» People bring children to Jesus and the disciples rebuke and try to stop them (Luke 18:15–17).

» A rich ruler asks Jesus how to inherit eternal life and the disciples do not interfere (Luke 18:18–30).

» Jesus once again predicts his death (Luke 18:31–34).

» A blind beggar cries out for Jesus to help him and the disciples rebuke him, telling him to be quiet (Luke 18:35–43).

» A tax collector climbs a tree to see Jesus and the disciples are silent (Luke 19:1–9).

Jesus taught on the power of persistent supplication, and then Luke recorded four pop quizzes for the disciples with children, a rich ruler, a blind beggar, and a tax collector, all of whom demonstrated persistence in their pursuit of Jesus. And how did the disciples respond? Not only did they not honor the children's and blind beggar's pursuit of Jesus, they made vigorous attempts to turn them away and silence them. However, no such resistance from the disciples is documented with regard to the rich ruler or tax collector. Granted, they might not have seen Zacchaeus up in the tree until it was too late, but Luke's record begs a question. As you reflect upon today's reading, list as many possibilities as you can of reasons why the disciples sought to silence and turn away children and a blind beggar from Jesus.

Today's Fast: Religious Profiling

Whom do we spiritually underestimate? The elderly? The young? The poor? The wealthy? The beautiful? The disabled? What group or class of people would we have turned away from Jesus? Are we guilty of classism, defined as "the belief that people can be distinguished or characterized, esp. as inferior, on the basis of their social class"?[2] Today, ask God to shine His light upon any form of religious profiling in which you are dismissing those Jesus would welcome.

On Lent

TABLE 2. POST-NICENE TEXTS REFERENCED IN SCHOLARSHIP
REGARDING THE ORIGIN OF LENT, PART ONE

APPROXIMATE DATES	ANCIENT WORK OR AUTHOR	KEY WORDS AND PHRASES
c. 335	St. Athanasius in his "Festal Letters" for the years 329–334[3] *Canons of Athanasius*	"holy fast," forty-day fast prior to Holy Week[4] forty days of penance fasting for readmission to Eucharist[5]
381–384	Egeria in *Itinerarium* 30.1 or *Egeria's Travels* [London 1971], pp. 128–39	forty-day fast,[6] "Great Week" distinct from rest of Lent[7]
385	Siricius, Bishop of Rome, letter to Himerius of Terragona in Spain	"forty-day" reference to a pre-paschal program for preparation of baptismal candidates[8]
387	St. John Chrysostom in Antioch in *Homilies on Genesis*, 30.1–3	forty days of fasting[9]
	Epiphanios for Cyprus	forty days of fasting[10]
	Augustine is baptized at the Easter Vigil April 24–25, 387[11]	

Today's Reading: John 14:1–14

_____

_____

_____

_____

_____

_____

_____

_____

_____

_____

_____

_____

_____

_____

DAY TWELVE

In celebration, the no-longer-blind beggar joyously followed Jesus into Jericho. Bartimaeus's praise must have been contagiously evident to all because Luke tells us that, "When all the people saw it, they also praised God" (Luke 18:43). Everyone the group passed heard the praise and witnessed the celebration. One soul in particular desperately wanted a clearer view of the Jesus at the center of the people's joy.

Imagine with me the now-sighted beggar standing near Jesus, as Jesus looked up into the sycamore tree and said, "Zacchaeus, come down immediately. I must stay at your house today" (Luke 19:5). We tend to read these stories as stand-alone narratives, but Bartimaeus and Zacchaeus were citizens of the same city. And though I feel rather confident stating that poor blind beggars and wealthy chief tax collectors did not eat at the same table, I have other questions that remain unanswered. Did Zacchaeus recognize Bartimaeus from the countless times he had walked past the same roadside? Did these two know each other's names? Did tax collection have anything to do with the beggar's poverty? Did Bartimaeus's praise inspire Zacchaeus to accept Jesus as the Messiah? Is it possible that the beggar helped make spiritually rich the man (or category of men) who made

> "It really boils down to this: that all life is interrelated. We are all caught in an inescapable network of mutuality, tied into a single garment of destiny. Whatever affects one directly, affects all indirectly. We are made to live together because of the interrelated structure of reality."
>
> —MARTIN LUTHER KING, JR. (1929–1968)[1]

him financially destitute? Was Bartimaeus among the recipients of Zacchaeus's exuberant, repentant act of restitution?

As I picture Jesus, Bartimaeus, and Zacchaeus celebrating the miracles of physical and spiritual sight, a reality resounds: though following Jesus is most often an individual act of faith, that act always has communal repercussions. We are interrelated. As one modern thinker has noted so eloquently, "*To be* is to inter-be. We cannot just be by ourselves alone."[2] Our stories, though unique, are woven of shared thread. I can only imagine the glorious tapestry Zacchaeus and Bartimaeus presented their city after that day when Jesus stood still at a roadside and then under a tree to welcome lost brothers home.

Reflection

Do you remember in school how we were instructed to utilize idea webs to sketch out essays? We placed ideas in circles and connected them to one another through lines to visually organize the story we wanted to tell. Mentally or on paper, draw a web of the people in your faith story.

Today's Fast: Isolation

Each holiday season, the classic *It's a Wonderful Life* warms hearts as we witness George Bailey's revelation of how his unapplauded Bedford Falls life has changed the world, one interconnected act of selfless kindness at a time. As George stands bewildered in front of his brother's tombstone, his angel explains:

> **Clarence:** Your brother, Harry Bailey, broke through the ice and was drowned at the age of nine.
> **George:** That's a lie! Harry Bailey went to war! He got the Congressional Medal of Honor! He saved the lives of every man on that transport!
> **Clarence:** Every man on that transport died. Harry wasn't there to save them because you weren't there to save Harry. Strange, isn't it? Each man's life touches so many other lives.[3]

And so we tear up when George realizes the vast network of people his valuable life has affected. We consider for a glowing moment the possibility that our lives also matter that profoundly. We smile as Clarence gets his wings . . . and then continue in our non-holiday isolated ways, underestimating the interconnectivity of humankind and life itself.

Almost two decades before the release of this classic film, Hungarian writer Frigyes Karinthy penned a short story in 1929 titled "Chain-Links," in which he postulated a theory that is now known as Six Degrees of Separation.[4] A key concept in city planning and social networking, the Six Degrees theory asserts that all humans can be connected by a maximum of six steps. Spiritually, the theory highlights the truth that each life needs and, in turn, affects all other lives.

Today, then, fast isolation. Meet a friend for coffee, call a cousin, visit a neighbor, or connect with a colleague. Purpose to link and be linked, to need and be needed, to see and be seen. Refuse to discount your influence, especially in seemingly small acts, and intentionally nurture your God-given web of relationships.

On Lent

TABLE 2. POST-NICENE TEXTS REFERENCED IN SCHOLARSHIP
REGARDING THE ORIGIN OF LENT, PART TWO

APPROXIMATE DATES	ANCIENT WORK OR AUTHOR	KEY WORDS AND PHRASES
c. 380–c. 450	Byzantine historian Socrates in *Historia Ecclesiastica 5.22*	"fasts before Easter," "three weeks excepting Saturdays and Sundays," "keeps the fast for six weeks," "Forty Days," "fast seven weeks before the feast"[5]
d. 444	St. Cyril of Alexandria in his "Festal Letters"	forty-day period of fasting[6]
d. 461	Pope St. Leo	"fulfill with their fasts the Apostolic institution of the forty days"[7]
late 4th C	*Apostolic Constitutions* (V.13.3–4)	fast "of the Holy Week of Pascha" after the forty-day fast[8]
5th C	Sozomen in *Histo. Eccl*, 7, 19	"the so-called Forty Days before Pascha . . . some begin at 6 weeks . . . others at 7 weeks."[9]

Today's Reading: John 14:15–22

_____

_____

_____

_____

_____

_____

_____

_____

_____

_____

_____

_____

_____

_____

_____

DAY THIRTEEN

Leaving Zacchaeus's joyful Jericho party behind them, Jesus and His disciples made their way to yet another dinner held in the home of Lazarus, Mary, and Martha. Bethany was Jesus' place of calm before the coming tempest. Arriving six days before the Passover, Jesus sat down at a dinner held in His honor, and:

> Mary took about a pint of pure nard, an expensive perfume; she poured it on Jesus' feet and wiped his feet with her hair. And the house was filled with the fragrance of the perfume. (John 12:3)

Each Gospel writer records an anointing of Jesus. In three of the four experiences, Jesus explained that the anointing was in preparation for His burial.[1] With details so similar, many over the centuries have viewed the accounts as different perspectives of the same story. However, the possibility exists that Jesus was actually anointed with expensive perfume three times during His public ministry. Consider the contrasts:

REFERENCE	TIME FRAME	VENUE	WOMAN	FOCUS	ET AL.
Mt 26:2, 6–13	2 days before the Passover, after Palm Sunday	Simon the Leper's home in Bethany	Unnamed	Jesus' head	The disciples were indignant
Mk 14:1–9	2 days before the Passover, after Palm Sunday	Simon the Leper's home in Bethany	Unnamed	Jesus' head	The disciples rebuke her harshly
Lk 7:36–50	Before John the Baptist was beheaded	Simon the Pharisee's home in Nain (?)	A sinful woman	Jesus' feet	Simon questions Jesus' discernment
Jn 12:1–8	6 days before the Passover, before Palm Sunday	Lazarus's home in Bethany	Mary	Jesus' feet	Judas objects

Two of these accounts were from eyewitnesses. Mark's and Matthew's versions obviously mirror each other. Luke was a historian. All of which currently leads me to a delightful hypothesis: in addition to being anointed early in His ministry (by a sinful woman who loved much because she had been forgiven much), Jesus was anointed twice during Passover Week in preparation for His burial. Six days before the Passover, a well-known woman, Mary, anointed His feet in her home, and two days before the Passover, an unnamed woman anointed His head at the home of Simon the Leper.

Which means that as He journeyed cross-ward, Jesus was—head to toe—rather smelly. Nard was serious stuff. The mob could have possibly just followed their noses to find Jesus in the olive grove. Well, perhaps that is an exaggeration, but Judas most likely would have been confronted by the perfume when he kissed Christ. And as Jesus hung on the cross, the fragrance would have reminded Him that Father God prepares all things well.

Reflection

Jesus spent a significant part of His last days at tables, resting in the company of old and new friends. If you had only six days to live, how, and with whom, would you live them? Why?

I am not moved, my God, to love you
By the heaven you have promised me.
Neither does hell, so feared, move me
To keep me from offending you.
You move me, Lord, and I am moved seeing you
Scoffed at and nailed on a cross.
I am moved seeing your body so wounded.
Your injuries and your death move me.
It is your love that moves me, and in such a way
that even though there were no heaven,
I would love you, and even though there were
no hell I would fear you.
You do not have to give me anything
so that I love you,
For even if I didn't hope for what I hope,
As I love you now, so would I love you.

—ANONYMOUS SPANISH POET,
OFTEN ATTRIBUTED TO JOHN OF
THE CROSS (1542–1591)[4]

Today's Fast: Stinginess

Pliny the Elder (AD 23–79), in his encyclopedic work, *Natural History*, mentions twelve species of nard.[2] Nard refers to thick essential oil created by crushing the roots of a plant that grows in the Himalayas of Nepal, China, and India.[3] The costliness of the ointment is attested to historically as well as in all scriptural occurrences:

The alabaster flask of ointment mentioned in the Gospels was a very costly one containing spikenard (*Nardostachys jatamansi*). This herb, related to valerian, was imported from North India and used widely by Hebrews and Romans alike in the anointing of the dead.[5]

Some of those present were saying indignantly to one another, "Why this waste of perfume? It could have been sold for more than a year's wages and the money given to the poor." And they rebuked her harshly. (Mark 14:4–5)

Why this waste? Because love does not calculate. What an honor: to be remembered as one who loved lavishly. Today, fast stinginess: seek an opportunity to be irrationally lavish toward someone who cannot possibly return the favor. Give because you love. Give without letting reason ration out your love in stingy portions.

On Lent

As previously mentioned, Table 1 and Table 2 together cite ancient documents and voices examined by scholars in their collective pursuit of the historical origins of Lent. Many of these sources were deemed relevant for the development of Lent specifically because they referenced fasting. However, consider the following far more ancient mention of fasting:

> "Even now," declares the LORD,
> > "return to me with all your heart,
> > with fasting and weeping and mourning." (Joel 2:12)

Joel, clearly, was not writing about Lent. I make this obvious point to emphasize that prior to the dawn of the church, fasting served multiple purposes in multiple contexts and, from God's perspective, was valuable to the extent that it reflected a posture of the heart.

As ministers and scholars of previous centuries sought to discern the early roots of Lent, an assumption guided some that ancient mentions of fasting were part of a larger discussion on preparation for baptism, and that the season preferred for baptism was Easter. Therefore, writings about fasting in general, and forty-day fasts in particular, were assumed to shed light upon the development of Lent. That assumption, however, is now considered quite questionable.

Today's Reading: John 14:23–31

DAY FOURTEEN

Leaving Bethany, Jesus' nard-adorned feet carried Him the short two-mile distance to Jerusalem. The apostle John described two distinct "crowds" that surrounded Jesus on what we now call Palm Sunday. The Greek word translated "crowds"—ὄχλος (*ochlos*)—referenced multitudes, large groups, or mobs consisting mostly of commoners—that is, not the ruling class.[1] The night before, in Bethany, as Jesus enjoyed the warmth of Lazarus's hospitality and Mary anointed His feet, "a large crowd of Jews found out that Jesus was there and came, not only because of him but also to see Lazarus, whom he had raised from the dead" (John 12:9). According to Luke's account, it seems that some part of this crowd—which Luke 19:37 further identified as a "crowd" of μαθητής (*mathētēs*), that is, "disciples"—followed Jesus into Jerusalem the next day.

Entering the City of David with a crowd of followers and disciples, Jesus was then further surrounded by a crowd already in the city. John explained, "The next day the great crowd that had come for the festival heard that Jesus was on his way to Jerusalem. They took palm branches and went out to meet him, shouting, 'Hosanna!'" (John 12:12–13). Around 550 years earlier, Zechariah had prophesied:

Rejoice greatly, Daughter Zion!

Shout, Daughter Jerusalem!

See, your king comes to you;

righteous and victorious,

lowly and riding on a donkey,

on a colt, the foal of a donkey. (Zechariah 9:9)

Though the disciples "did not understand all this" until "after Jesus was glorified,"[2] Jesus, in fulfillment of the prophecy, entered Jerusalem riding a borrowed colt and as the crowd of His followers met the crowd at the Feast, messianic joy erupted! The scene that followed still inspires celebration when remembered two thousand years later. For a moment, for one beautiful moment, the crowds of Jerusalem honored their King. Covering the road in a royal carpet of palm branches and cloaks, the multitude shouted messianic praises: "Hosanna to the Son of David! Blessed is he who comes in the name of the Lord! Hosanna in the highest heaven!" (Matthew 21:9).

> "Come, let us go up together to the Mount of Olives to meet Christ who is returning today from Bethany and going of His own accord to that holy and blessed Passion to complete the mystery of our salvation. Let us imitate those who have gone out to meet Him, not scattering olive branches or garments or palms in His path, but spreading ourselves before Him as best we can, with humility of soul and upright purpose. So may we welcome the Word as He comes, so may God, who cannot be contained within any bounds, be contained within us."
>
> —ANDREW OF CRETE (AD 660–740)[3]

And Jesus did not stop them.

In fact, when anxious leaders told Jesus to rebuke his fans, Jesus said, "If they keep quiet, the stones will cry out" (Luke 19:39–40). Within a few short days, some of these same voices would exchange shouts of "Hosanna!" for shouts of "Crucify him!" Yet, even though He knew that the people would soon reject Him, Jesus still showed up for the parade they held in His honor. Jesus did not let the rejection of tomorrow cause Him to reject the love of today.

Reflection

Activate your God-given imagination to picture Jesus riding on a colt into Jerusalem. See the crowds of followers and disciples with Him and rush to meet Him with the crowd that had gathered for the feast. Decide whether you will be among those who throw their only cloak on the ground for His colt to walk upon. Observe the objecting leaders. Hear the shouts of children. Add your voice to the cries of "Hosanna!" Taste the messianic anticipation and then look into Jesus' eyes. What emotions might you have witnessed as He journeyed into the City of David?

Today's Fast: Spectatorship

The religious leaders were aghast on Palm Sunday with the crowds, the cloaks, the palm branches, and the praise. "Teacher, rebuke your disciples!" they demanded (Luke 19:39). The whole celebration was too wild, too organic, too out of their control. So they refused to enter in and sacrificed joy to something they deemed greater—be that propriety, suspicion, or, perhaps, jealousy. I wonder if I, too, would have paused, because I am by nature overly cautious. Organic inspires me, but spontaneous? Well, at times, the combination of troubleshooting, discernment, and introversion reduces me to a spectator instead of a participant. I, too, can hesitate and sacrifice participation to overthink. Today, fast spiritual spectatorship. Enter into worship. When considerations start turning into hesitations about something Jesus is clearly at the center of, throw hypercaution to the wind, and celebrate Jesus with abandon.

On Lent

In addition to the assumption that ancient mentions of fasting were linked with Easter via baptism, many earlier scholars also assumed that Lent's origins were apostolic. Highly respected spiritual leaders and scholars affirmed the apostolic roots of Lent, including Robert Bellarmine[4] (1542–1621), Bishop Lancelot Andrewes[5] (1555–1626), John Cosin[6] (1594–1572), Herman Lilienthal Lonsdale[7] (1858–1940), and in 2006, Fr. William P. Saunders[8] (1957–). Since the spiritual grandson of the apostle John (Ireneaus) spoke of fasts in connection to Resurrection Sunday and referred to varying practices dating back to the time of his "ancestors,"[9] Russo explains that:

> Many of the theology handbooks of the nineteenth and early-twentieth century confidently claimed that Lent was established by the apostles themselves or in the immediate post-apostolic period at the latest. They assumed this season of fasting was closely connected with preparation for Easter baptisms—a practice likewise considered to be of apostolic foundation (cf. Romans 6) and observed everywhere throughout the Church since its earliest days.[10]

Today's Reading: John 15:1–17

_____

_____

_____

_____

_____

DAY FIFTEEN

Yesterday we pictured Jesus riding on the colt through Jerusalem with exuberant crowds shouting "Hosanna!" Recall what emotions He might have experienced. Surely few of us picture Him stern and stoic, ignoring the joy all around Him, or anxious and jittery, waiting for the other shoe to drop, or rolling His eyes in dismissal of the nonsense. I picture Jesus smiling, looking around Him at the radiant faces of the Twelve and the hope-filled eyes of the masses. Knowing that the Twelve would soon run for their lives and the masses would soon reject Him, Jesus still stayed fully present for the party.

This quality of Christ strikes me as utterly remarkable. Honestly, I probably would have silenced all except for the small group of Jesus' faithful followers, but not for the reasons that motivated the Pharisees. I would have insulated myself from the crowds' favor because their favor would soon falter: crowds are fickle that way. In contrast, throughout His ministry and in amplified form during His Passion Week, Jesus consistently displayed an ability to receive from people in the moment what He knew would not endure.

In the Triumphal Entry, Jesus permitted the crowd's support, knowing it would soon sour. Jesus still lovingly and fully affirmed Peter's future leadership immediately after prophesying Peter's denial. Jesus still welcomed Judas to the communion table, knowing that betrayal was in his heart. In short, Jesus did not emotionally self-protect. His love did not shrink back even when His love—for a moment or, sadly, for a lifetime—would ultimately be rejected.

Lent mentors us in following Christ's example. As we consider Jesus' response to suffering, we become attentive to our own. Psychiatrist Anthony Reading explains that in relationships in general, "Individuals who have been hurt by lost hopes tend to protect themselves against future disappointment by lowering their sights and dimming their aspirations."[2] The same is true in our relationship with God. Uncertain that God will protect us, we proactively protect ourselves. To avoid further emotional and theological pain, we lower our expectations, edit our dreams, and shrink back from God through fear-driven planning, endless worry, hypervigilance, or the numbing of hope. With each choice to self-protect, another layer is added to insulate our hearts from attentiveness to God's presence. Rowan Williams notes, "In suffering, the believer's self-protection and isolation are broken."[3] This is a sacred work of our Lenten journey cross-ward, because our deepest self-protective defaults can often only be exposed, examined, and abandoned through suffering.

> "A direct experience of union or deep intimacy may be beautiful beyond words, but it also requires a certain sacrifice of our self-image as separate and distinct. We become vulnerable, less in control. We can no longer maintain the illusion that we are the master of our destiny."
>
> —GERALD G. MAY[1]

With all our inconsistencies, God does not shrink back from us. In turn, may we seek to never shrink back from God.

Reflection

Actions reveal beliefs because beliefs inspire actions. Consider Jesus' choice at the Triumphal Entry, knowing all that was to come. What must Jesus have believed in order to stay present to the party?

Today's Fast: Spiritual Self-Protection

Self-protection is not always unhealthy. For instance, when we brace ourselves for an impending car accident or run when chased by an angry animal, we are instinctively self-protecting our physical bodies. Even some forms of emotional self-protection are healthy, such as when we self-differentiate from a toxic relative. Self-protection in these examples is a response to danger: we self-protect when we do not feel safe. Therefore, when we spiritually self-protect, is it because we do not feel safe with God?

He is, after all, rather big and unpredictable and "wild, you know. Not like a tame lion."⁴ But I venture a guess that our disappointments fuel this unhealthy form of self-protection more than does His wildness. Spiritual leaders in our lives have abused power, prayer requests have gone unanswered, dreams have died, others experienced greater results for the same spiritual efforts, stepping out in faith backfired . . . and so we maintain a polite distance from deeper levels of intimacy with God. God said of His people that He had "engraved [them] on the palm of [His] hands" (Isaiah 49:16). Well, we conclude, He may write the names of His favorites on His hands, but we suspect that He has our initials somewhere less favored, like the back of His left heel.

Crazily enough, favor is not what frees us from self-protection: suffering is. Not suffering itself, but the choice within suffering to trust, to hope, and to love. Fasting self-protective habits is a lifetime commitment, but today we can take a step. Today, ask the Holy Spirit to alert you when you are shrinking back from God. Take note of the situation and later attempt to process the "why?" This is an exercise that you can carry with you daily throughout the Lenten season as we continue to see how pain, for Jesus, prompted an increase, not a decrease, in His vulnerability toward man and His heavenly Father.

On Lent

Whereas some believed that the apostles honored a forty-day Lenten fast, others believed that the forty-day fast grew gradually from an apostolic tradition of a one-day, two-day, or forty-hour fast such as referenced by Irenaeus and Tertullian.[5] According to this theory, these shorter, pre-Easter fasts—coinciding with Jesus' time in the tomb—then evolved into the pre-Nicene mention of a six-day pre-paschal fast.[6] This in turn evolved into a "three-week fast before baptism . . . [and a] six-week fast for catechumens that would be baptized on the Feast of the Resurrection"[7] (thirty-six days—six weeks minus Sundays—being considered by some as a "tithe" of the year).[8] Finally, an extra four days were added to arrive at a forty-day Lenten fast[9]—forty being a number weighted with biblical significance. This hypothesis came to be known as the *backwards extension* theory.[10]

Today's Reading: John 15:18–16:4

_____

_____

_____

_____

_____

_____

_____

_____

_____

_____

_____

_____

_____

_____

_____

_____

DAY SIXTEEN

Jesus' emotions and actions in the days following the Triumphal Entry were something less (far less) than placid. He wept over Jerusalem, forcefully cleared the temple, cursed a fig tree, confounded religious leaders, told pointed parables, and experienced emotional distress. This is not the carefree Jesus with soft backlit curls and spotless, wrinkle-free garments sitting beside a bubbling brook depicted in the old family Bible. Frankly, I like this Jesus better and I am going to guess that you do too. But in order for us to let Jesus be Jesus, we must make room in His life, and in our own, for a broader range of emotions and actions in our working definition of *holy*.

Holy grieves. (Think: ugly cry.) Embedded in his account of the Triumphal Entry, Luke relays Jesus' guttural response when He sees the city of Jerusalem: Jesus wept at the sight. Luke chose the word κλαίω (*klaiō*) to express Jesus' grief. Also translated *lament, wail,* and *cry, klaiō* is used to express "grief at parting, remorse, [and] sorrow for the dead."[1] *Klaiō* is a mourning cry. When the King on a colt saw Jerusalem, He wailed:

If you, even you, had only known on this day what would bring you peace—but now it is hidden from your eyes. The days will come upon you when your enemies will build an embankment against you and encircle you and hem you in on every side. They will dash you to the ground, you and the children within your walls. They will not leave one stone on another, because you did not recognize the time of God's coming to you. (Luke 19:42–44)

Jesus treasured the City of David. When He was eight days old, Jesus entered Jerusalem for the first time to be circumcised, and the elders Simeon and Anna recognized Him as the Messiah. But now, over thirty years later, Jesus entered the city to be crucified, and the elders would recognize Him not. Jesus grieved for a people who would not know peace. Jesus grieved for the city that would pay for its spiritual blindness with destruction. *Holy grieves.*

> "[Jesus cries,] 'Jerusalem, Jerusalem, you who kill the prophets and stone those sent to you, how often I have longed to gather your children together, as a hen gathers her chicks under her wings, and you were not willing.' God holds back; he hides himself; he weeps. Why? Because he desires what power can never win. He is a king who wants not subservience, but love. Thus, rather than mowing down Jerusalem, Rome, and every other worldly power, he chose the slow, hard way of Incarnation, love, and death. A conquest from within."
>
> —PHILIP YANCEY[2]

Reflection

The word translated *wept* in Luke 19 is the same word Jesus used in the Beatitudes when He said, "Blessed are you who weep now" (Luke 6:21). Recall any personal moments in your life when weeping was "blessed."

Today's Fast: Halos

Halos, coiffured hair, and even the beloved "Away in the Manger"'s "no crying he makes" reflect our theological struggle with Jesus' incarnation. What does it mean to be holy *and* human? Though I respect the purpose and appreciate the symbolism of nimbuses in religious art, when the "Word became flesh and made his dwelling among us" (John 1:14), He was not born with a halo. Of course He cried. Crying is not sin. Of course He did not have perfect backlit hair. Messy is not sin.

One of the reasons we must wrestle with the mystery of the Incarnation is because if we are not seasoned with the wrestling, we tend to offer utterly unhelpful things to others and to ourselves, such as, "You shouldn't cry, grieve, wail, or weep. God is in control. He works all things for the good of those who love Him . . . so there's no need to feel _____." No one understood God's goodness and control more than Jesus, and He still wept. Which means we can too.

Today, fast the halos of false definitions of holy. Ask God where He is weeping in your life and in the world and join Him there. It is never weakness to grieve where God is grieving.

On Lent

Along with the apostolic roots of Lent, the backwards extension theory seemed sound until research called into question the historical integrity of the bridge connecting fasting and baptism to Easter. Several scholars reconsidered key premises upon which previous theories had been based. After discussing evidence from Rome, Jerusalem, Spain, North Africa, Naples, and Constantinople, Maxwell Johnson (cited in many of the peer-reviewed articles[3] as a leading source on this issue) concluded that "in its origins, therefore,

'Lent' has nothing to do with Easter at all but everything to do with the final training of candidates for baptism."[4] Orthodox scholars John Paul Abdelsayed and Moses Samaan agreed:

> It is now believed that the theory of a single origin of the Great Lent cannot be sustained. It is more likely that the emergence of the pre-Paschal Lent is due to the fusion and confusion of several pre-Nicene patterns of fasting, penitence, and pre-baptismal preparation.[5]

Today's Reading: John 16:5–16

_____

_____

_____

_____

_____

_____

_____

_____

_____

_____

DAY SEVENTEEN

Not only does holy grieve, *holy gets angry.* Like you, I have heard masterful sermons explaining the "why" of Jesus' temple clearing. At the age of twelve, Jesus called the temple "my Father's house" (Luke 2:49), so as an adult the Father's only Son came to put that house in order. The moneychangers had set up their tables in the Court of the Gentiles, thus turning the very space that enabled the temple to be "a house of prayer for all nations" (Isaiah 56:7) into a "den of robbers" (Jeremiah 7:11). So Jesus purged the temple in fulfillment of prophecy (Malachi 3:2), confronting religious corruption that profited and prospered at the expense of the poor and the foreigner.

For our Lenten journey, instead of considering in greater depth the more commonly addressed *why* of the temple clearing, we will focus upon the far-less-comfortable *how* of the temple clearing. Jesus was upset by what He saw in the temple and He responded with physical protest. Scholarly consensus leans toward two temple clearings: one at the beginning of Jesus' public ministry (recounted by John) and one at the end (attested by Matthew, Mark, and Luke.) I have drawn from both events to detail the holy "how" of the temple clearing. As you read, imagine yourself in the temple that day.

» "So he **made a whip** out of cords..." (John 2:15)
» "...and **began driving out** those who were buying and selling there." (Mark 11:15)[1]
» "...he **scattered the coins** of money changers..." (John 2:15)
» "He **overturned the tables** of the money changers and the benches of those selling doves." (Matthew 21:12)[2]
» "...and [he] **would not allow anyone to carry merchandise** through the temple courts." (Mark 11:16)
» He said, "**Get these out of here!** Stop turning my Father's house into a market!" (John 2:16)[3]

How would you have felt about Jesus in the temple that day if you were a Gentile? A moneychanger? A religious leader? His disciple? Does what you imagine sync with your definition of *sinless*? If not, your definition may be too small. *Holy gets angry.* So does this mean we need to buy ropes and start making whips? No. But perhaps we need to stop hiding safely behind hashtag campaigns and instead show up and speak out. And perhaps the next time we feel angry about corruption and injustice, instead of stifling the anger, we should ask God what He wants us to do with the anger. Odds are, He probably feels angry too.

> "Joy and sadness are born at the same time, both arising from such deep places in your heart that you can't find words to capture your complex emotions. But this intimate experience in which every bit of life is touched by a bit of death can point us beyond the limits of our existence."
>
> —HENRI NOUWEN (1932–1996)[4]

Reflection

Jesus' first visit to the temple was on the eighth day for His circumcision. Thereafter His family would have returned each year for Passover.

Moneychangers were in the area with vendors who sold animals, birds, and other items used in temple worship and sacrifices. Such transactions were numerous and required the service of brokers who knew the value of foreign money. Some exchangers profited greatly and loaned their money along with what others invested with them. Their interest rates ranged from 20 to 300 percent per year.[5]

This practice was not new. Jesus witnessed the corruption for years as faithful believers from outside Judea journeyed to the temple and exchanged their currency for the required temple shekel at unfair rates. Why do you think Jesus waited to address the injustice?

Today's Fast: Apathy

apathy, n. /ˈæpəθɪ/ Freedom from, or insensibility to, suffering; hence, freedom from, or insensibility to, passion or feeling; passionless existence.[6]

Apathy describes an emotional disconnect from life in general and suffering in particular. In a society drowning in bad "news," apathy can seem an attractive alternative to absorbing the insane amount of planetary pain that the Internet brings to our attention every waking moment. However, the antonyms of *apathy* are not *absorption, activism,* or even *emotionalism*: they are *sympathy, sensitivity,* and *concern*.[7]

> He has shown you, O mortal, what is good.
> And what does the LORD require of you?
> To act justly and to love mercy
> and to walk humbly with your God. (Micah 6:8)

What then is our responsibility as concerned—that is, non-apathetic—Jesus-followers when we witness injustice? The fact that Jesus witnessed injustice in the temple courts years before His protest affirms that timing matters.[8] Taking action because there is a need is a very different motivation than taking action because there is a God. In addition to being exhausting, the former is led by what our eyes see and what our hearts feel. The latter is led by loving listening and dependence-inspired discipline.

A dear friend, Dr. Beth Grant, once said, "Choose carefully what you are willing to die for because you can only die once."[9] Jesus, no doubt, witnessed many injustices during His life on earth, but He did not turn over many tables. As we fast apathy today, let us ask God to awaken us from our numb slumber and reveal to us His *where, when,* and *how* of any tables that need to be overthrown in our generation.

On Lent

How did centuries of semi-certainty regarding the historical development of Lent dissolve? Allow me to quote at length from the excellent work of Russo:

First, scholars no longer take for granted the antiquity and ubiquity of Paschal baptism. Tertullian, admittedly, indicates that Easter was a "most solemn day for baptism," but he is only one of a handful of writers in the pre-Nicene period (that is, before AD 325) who indicates this preference and even he says that Easter was by no means the only favored day for baptisms in his locale. Easter baptism does not become widespread until the mid-fourth century . . .

Second, the fasts observed before baptism described in many pre-Nicene sources are no longer presumed to be pre-paschal or related in any way to Lent. . . . Previously, scholars assumed these and other pre-baptismal fasts were pre-paschal and related to, if not identical with, the early Lent. With Easter baptism no longer the ancient and widespread custom once thought, these baptismal fasts too were reexamined.

Rather than being part of a proto-Lent, they are now interpreted simply as free-floating periods of fasting undertaken whenever baptisms were administered.

Third, developing research on Holy Week and the Triduum has shown that these periods are not the cores of a gradually lengthening pre-Easter fast, but are actually separate periods to which the forty-day Lent has been joined or overlaps.[10]

In other words, if fasting is most often associated with baptism but baptism is not always associated with Easter, then the bridge is out between ancient mentions of fasts and Resurrection Sunday.

Today's Reading: John 16:17–33

_____

_____

_____

_____

_____

_____

_____

_____

DAY EIGHTEEN

Early in the morning, as he was on his way back to the city, he was hungry. Seeing a fig tree by the road, he went up to it but found nothing on it except leaves. Then he said to it, "May you never bear fruit again!" Immediately the tree withered.
—MATTHEW 21:18–19[1]

In the morning, as they went along, they saw the fig tree withered from the roots. Peter remembered and said to Jesus, "Rabbi, look! The fig tree you cursed has withered!"
—MARK 11:20–21

*H*oly . . . *curses?* Yes, I searched the thesaurus: a more palatable synonym does not exist. Yes, taken out of context this could be disastrous. Yes, even within the context, this is troublesome. This was Jesus' only "destructive miracle."[2] The word that is translated *curse,* καταράομαι (*kataraomai*), appears four additional times in the New Testament as follows:

» In the parable of the sheep and the goats: "Then he will say to those on his left, 'Depart from me, you who are cursed, into the eternal fire prepared for the devil and his angels'" (Matthew 25:41).

» Jesus teaching on loving one's enemies: "Bless those who curse you" (Luke 6:28).

» Paul teaching on love: "Bless those who persecute you; bless and do not curse" (Romans 12:14).

» On taming the tongue: "With the tongue we praise our Lord and Father, and with it we curse human beings, who have been made in God's likeness . . . this should not be" (James 3:9–10).

So, being cursed is a bad thing.[3] Clearly, we should never curse humans. If people curse us, we are to bless them instead of responding in kind. And, Jesus cursed the poor fig tree. Why? Certainly the fig tree's withering demonstrated the sheer authority of Jesus' voice and Jesus used the event to teach the disciples about the power of believing prayer.[4] But additionally, some scholars believe that the fig tree was the unfortunate prop in one of Jesus' more vivid illustrated sermons on the fate of His fruitless nation.[5]

Matthew and Mark positioned the fig tree incident after the temple clearing and immediately preceding a confrontation in which the religious leaders (who obviously had not seen the fig tree yet) questioned Jesus' authority. Following that confrontation, Jesus shared a series of parables, many of which contained thinly veiled commentaries on the religious leaders' lack of fruitfulness. At that time of year, fig trees would be filled with green leaves and unripe, green, disagreeable fruit.[6] However, this green, leafy fig tree had no fruit whatsoever.

> The Lenten spring has come
> the light of repentance!
> O brothers, let us cleanse ourselves from all evil,
> crying out to the Giver of Light:
> Glory to Thee, O Lover of man.
>
> —TRADITIONAL ORTHODOX HYMN[7]

While Jesus did not expect the fruit to be ripe, He did expect the fruit to exist and to be in formation.

His judgment on the fig tree echoed His sobering words for those who refuse to remain in Him:

If a man remains in me and I in him, he will bear much fruit; apart from me you can do nothing. If anyone does not remain in me, he is like a branch that is thrown away and withers; such branches are picked up, thrown into the fire and burned. (John 15:5–6)

Jesus, evidently, finds utter fruitlessness frustrating.

Reflection

Read Luke 13:6–9 below. Consider the parallels between this parable and Jesus' judgment upon the fig tree.

Then he told this parable: "A man had a fig tree, planted in his vineyard, and he went to look for fruit on it, but did not find any. So he said to the man who took care of the vineyard, 'For three years now I've been coming to look for fruit on this fig tree and haven't found any. Cut it down! Why should it use up the soil?' 'Sir,' the man replied, 'leave it alone for one more year, and I'll dig around it and fertilize it. If it bears fruit next year, fine! If not, then cut it down.'"

Today's Fast: Appearances

In an early confrontation with the Pharisees and teachers of the law, Jesus quoted Isaiah 29:13 and said: "You hypocrites! Isaiah was right when he prophesied about you: 'These people honor me with their lips, but their hearts are far from me. They worship me in vain; their teachings are merely human rules" (Matthew 15:7–9). Consistently throughout Scripture, God expresses His frustration with religiosity. The appearance of faith without the fruit of faith and worshipful words without a worship-filled heart are, in Jesus' words, "vain."

Today, fast all appearances. Fast facades. Be fiercely attentive to when, where, and with whom you are tempted to inflate or deflate, exaggerate, or belittle your real self via speech or silence. Discuss your observations with Jesus. Ask Him to help you understand why you are investing energy in an illusion. Our reality does not frustrate Jesus. Our hypocrisy does.

On Lent

What then remains in our search for the origins of Lent? Russo poses three options: 1) Lent inexplicably appeared as a new custom after the Council of Nicea; 2) The "alleged Egyptian post-Theophany fast" was the "dominant antecedent to Lent;" or 3) Lent grew from a fusion of several different fasts.[8] In my research, I found no proponents of option one. However, among the scholars who acknowledged the collapse of earlier, simpler, backward extension Lenten origin theories, most shared rather strong agreement on the prominent role baptismal preparation played in the origins of what came to be known as Lent. On Lent's continuing connection with baptism, Schmemann's words are simply beautiful:

> But even when the Church rarely baptized adults and the institution of the catechumenate disappeared, the basic meaning of Lent remained the same. For even though we are baptized, what we constantly lose and betray is precisely that which we received at Baptism. Therefore, Easter is our return every year to our own Baptism, whereas Lent is our preparation for that return—the slow and sustained effort to perform, at the end, our own 'passage' or 'pascha' into the new life in Christ.[9]

Today's Reading: John 17:1–5

_____

_____

_____

_____

_____

_____

_____

_____

_____

_____

_____

_____

_____

DAY NINETEEN

*H*oly is feisty. If *feisty* stretches you too much, feel free to substitute *spirited* or *plucky*. All three are apropos to describe Jesus' retort to the chief priests and elders when they questioned His credentials. Increasingly huffy about Jesus' escalating influence, these leaders challenged Jesus to identify the source of His authority.

> Jesus entered the temple courts, and, while he was teaching, the chief priests and the elders of the people came to him. "By what authority are you doing these things?" they asked. "And who gave you this authority?" (Matthew 21:23)

Jesus responded to their question with another question, and I see more in His strategy than a nod to the Socratic method of discussion. Of all the recorded interactions of Jesus, this is the only time Jesus instituted if-then ground rules. He said, "I will also ask you one question. If you answer me, I will tell you by what authority I am doing these things" (Matthew 21:24).

Peer to peer, we might frame this interaction as a lively debate. But from a poor, thirty-something Nazarene to the rich, religious, ruling class in Jerusalem? As I said, holy is feisty. Jesus made answering the leaders' question conditional upon the leaders answering whether John's baptism was "from heaven, or of human origin" (Matthew 21:25). In addition to linking Himself with John's message and ministry, Jesus'

> "The question asked is not, 'What should be happening in my life?' but 'What is happening in my life?' The present moment, the present set of circumstances, the present relationships in our lives—this is where God lives. This is where God meets us and gives us life."
>
> —ALICE FRYLING[1]

challenge exposed a disconnect between inquiry and honesty in these leaders' lives. Placing their well-groomed heads together, the leaders pondered their dilemma:

> They discussed it among themselves and said, "If we say, 'From heaven,' he will ask, 'Then why didn't you believe him?' But if we say, 'Of human origin'—we are afraid of the people, for they all hold that John was a prophet." So they answered Jesus, "We don't know." (Matthew 21:25–27)

The chief priests and elders processed Jesus' question like a game of chess, calculating the outcomes of potential moves. When they could not figure out how to secure an advantageous position, they abdicated their turn and said, "We don't know." They thought strategically, but not honestly. They examined "Where do we want to end up?" but not "What do we believe to be true?" When the leaders refused to answer—let alone to answer honestly—Jesus also issued a refusal: "Neither will I tell you by what authority I am doing these things" (Matthew 21:27).[2] These leaders valued positioning more than truth, and Jesus closed the question.

I repeat: Jesus closed the question.

Evidently, valuing something more than truth limits our interaction with Jesus. Taken seriously, this is rather sobering. Do we value something more than truth? Have control and position become more precious to us than sincerity? Are we committed to the pursuit of emotional and intellectual honesty in God's presence? Jesus did not ask the leaders for polite acquiescence or polished theology. He simply asked them to be true.

Reflection

Lent is a time to ask ourselves if we, like the leaders in Matthew 21, value anything more than truth. Is Jesus awaiting honesty from us? Is there any question Jesus could ask that we would rather not answer?

Today's Fast: Revisionism

Have you ever interacted with a chronic revisionist? The motivational root of revisionism seems to be either the fear of losing power or the compulsion to avoid pain. Both are pursuits of control. Pain-avoiders change the story to absolve themselves from responsibility: they revise history because the weight of reality is too crushing to bear. Power-seekers, such as the above religious leaders, revise history to maintain their dominant status. Either way, revisionism starts with a desired outcome and then works backward to fabricate an origin story. In other words, "truth" is created retroactively—which, obviously, makes it no truth at all.

Revisionism is a deadly form of self-deception and a formidable foe of intimacy with God. Today, be brutally honest with yourself: are you spinning the real story to your advantage? Have you grown comfortable with "white lies"? Do you find yourself exaggerating or underestimating reality? Why? May God help us all, this Lenten season and beyond, to walk in truth.

On Lent

Allow me at this point to return to my personal musings from Day One. *Which came first, the discipline of fasting or the journey of Lent? Did they grow up together? Did one mature into the other? Are they two distinct experiences that fused over time?* From this vantage point, it appears that in origin, Lent—as an extended period of fasting—is more related to preparing for baptism than preparing for Easter. Ancient pre-baptismal fasts originally grew independently of Easter and have remained an integral part of Lenten observance even long after their ancient baptismal context lessened in universal emphasis. Therefore, though from apostolic times there has been a period of preparation for Easter, Lent, as we know it today as a forty-day season of fasting, emerged through a separate but still sacred and sober remembrance of John the Baptist's cries by the waters of the Jordan River:

> Repent, for the kingdom of heaven has come near. (Matthew 3:2)
> I baptize you with water for repentance. But after me will come one who is more powerful than I, whose sandals I am not worthy to carry. He will baptize you with the Holy Spirit and with fire. (Matthew 3:11)
> Make straight the way for the Lord. (John 1:23)

Today's Reading: John 17:6–19

_____

_____

_____

_____

_____

_____

_____

_____

_____

_____

_____

_____

_____

_____

DAY TWENTY

B etween this point and the accounts of the Last Supper, the Gospel writers devoted the majority of their ink to the retelling of Jesus' final parables and teachings. One-third of Jesus' parables and two-thirds of Jesus' teachings during this critical Passion Week space were spoken to or directed at religious leaders. After He closed the question posed by the chief priests and elders, Jesus opened a few questions of His own via the Parable of the Two Sons and the Parable of the Tenants. Teaching in the temple courts, Jesus told the story of a father who asked his two sons to go work in his vineyard. One son said "yes" and lived "no," while the second son said "no" and lived "yes." Jesus then asked: "Which of the two did what his father wanted?" (Matthew 21:31) When the leaders verbalized the obvious, Jesus linked His new question with their closed one and said:

> Truly I tell you, the tax collectors and the prostitutes are entering the kingdom of God ahead of you. For John came to you to show you the way of righteousness, and you did not believe him, but the tax

collectors and the prostitutes did. And even after you saw this, you did not repent and believe him. (Matthew 21:31–32)

In His response, Jesus answered His own question clearly: was John's baptism from heaven or from men? It was from heaven. Further, those who repented after listening to John showed themselves to be God's obedient children.

Before the leaders could regroup, Jesus told them another parable that was even more pointed. A landowner rented his well-situated vineyard to some farmers. Yet when he sent his servants to collect what was due him, the tenants beat, stoned, and killed them. Finally, the landowner sent his son, hoping that he would be respected, but the tenants killed the heir as well. Then Jesus boldly asked the leaders what the owner would do to such tenants. Seemingly oblivious to whom they were in the story, the leaders replied, "He will bring those wretches to a wretched end . . . and he will rent the vineyard to other tenants" (Matthew 21:41). So Jesus spoke plainly: "I tell you that the kingdom of God will be taken away from you and given to a people who will produce its fruit" (Matthew 21:43). "When the chief priests and the Pharisees heard Jesus' parables, they knew he was talking about them" (Matthew 21:45).

Holy rebukes. And this was just a warm-up to the painfully public critique Jesus made of the teachers of the law and Pharisees recorded in Matthew 23. Jesus' message rang clear in this interim: God's love language is not words alone. We can talk all we want, but at the end of the day, we will also be judged by what we *did*. "Where then is mercy?" some might

> "It seems that what St. Basil identified as a danger lurking behind some of the practices of late antiquity, namely the dangers of isolationism, individualism, and self-pleasing, still remain. The temptation of our own time seems to be the same, a spirituality focused upon the self as its ultimate *telos*."
>
> —GEORGE KALENTZIS[1]

ask. For Jesus' disciples then and today, mercy is inherent within Jesus' rebukes because to hear them is to still have breath to respond to them with repentance.

Reflection

Oh, if this book were titled *100 Days of Decrease* I would have loved to linger in each parable and teaching! Select a parable or one of the teachings below aimed specifically at the religious leaders and ask God to give you the strength to find yourself in the story.

TABLE 3: PARABLES AND TEACHINGS DIRECTED TOWARD RELIGIOUS RULERS BETWEEN THE QUESTIONING OF JESUS AND THE LAST SUPPER

PARABLES

	MATTHEW	MARK	LUKE	JOHN
Parable of the Two Sons	21:28–32			
Parable of the Tenants	21:33–44	12:1–12	20:9–18	
Parable of the Wedding Banquet	22:1–14		14:16–24	
Parable of the Wise Servant	24:45–51	13:34–37		
Parable of the Pharisee and the Tax Collector			18:9–14	
Parable of the Ten Virgins	25:1–13			
Parable of the Talents	25:14–30		19:12–27	
Parable of the Fig Tree			21:29–36	
Parable of the Sheep and Goats	25:31–46			
Parable of the Seed				12:24

TEACHINGS

	MATTHEW	MARK	LUKE	JOHN
On the coming of the Kingdom of God			17:20–37	
On what is good			18:18–30	
On paying taxes to Caesar	22:19–22	12:13–17	20:20–26	
On marriage after the resurrection	22:23–33	12:18–27	20:27–40	
On the greatest commandment	22:34–40	12:28–34		
On whose Son is the Christ	22:41–46	12:35–37	20:41–44	
On seven woes	23:1–32	12:38–40	20:45–47	
On the widow's offering		12:41–44	21:1–4	
On Jesus' lament for Jerusalem	23:33–39		13:34–35	
On signs of the end of the age	24:1–44	13:1–37	21:5–36	
On walking in the light				12:35–36

Today's Fast: Leavened Bread

During the Exodus, God's people hurriedly left Egypt and "took their dough before the yeast was added" (Exodus 12:34). Yeast became a symbol of what was to be left behind in Egypt: hypocrisy, corruption, and bondage. Post-Exodus, "possibly because fermentation implied disintegration and corruption, leaven was excluded from all offerings placed on the altar to be sacrificed to God."[2] Jesus used leaven as a metaphor of false teaching and hypocrisy: "Be on your guard against the yeast of the Pharisees, which is hypocrisy" (Luke 12:1). And to this day during the Jewish Passover, leavened breads are fasted to commemorate the Israelites' deliverance from slavery.

Today, I invite you to fast leavened breads as a symbol of rejecting hypocrisy. Feel free to take up the challenge of buying or making unleavened breads, or simply fast flour entirely. Before each leaven-free meal, pause quietly and ask God to search your heart for any remnants of hypocrisy.

On Lent

Today we transition from an examination of the historical origins of Lent to an exploration of historical practices of Lent. One of my most delightful discoveries in writing *40 Days of Decrease* was the mosaic of practices associated with Lenten observance. Obviously, not all practices were manifest in all ages by all who honored Lent. Of Lent's many traditions, only a few—most of which were more frequently substantiated in the research[3] and some of which I simply found interesting—will be considered in the coming days. Space and time limit all that could be considered in this area, so allow me to preempt disappointment in the not-remotely-exhaustive nature of what follows.

First, it is well beyond the scope of this work to create a time line for each practice (though such a chronology would be fascinating). Second, in the same way, it is also sadly beyond the scope of this work to contrast the practices and liturgy of the Eastern Orthodox[4] and Western Roman Catholic churches preceding and following the Great Schism of AD 1054.[5] Third, with the exception of few brief (and more interesting) exceptions, I have left a comprehensive review of the vast amount of information awaiting organization and presentation on the myriad of methods, motives, and variations of food-fasting practices over the last two thousand years to another book . . . and another author. (It would make a fascinating dissertation. Let me know if you write it.)

Today's Reading: John 17:20–26

_____

_____

_____

_____

_____

_____

_____

_____

_____

_____

_____

_____

_____

DAY TWENTY-ONE

Jesus (our pure Redeemer) experienced grief, anger, and frustration. Jesus (our sinless Savior) cursed fig trees, turned over tables of injustice, and issued public rebukes to hypocrites. Which brings us to John 12:27 and another window into Jesus' holy—but not remotely dull—inner world.

Either Hellenistic Jews or God-fearing Gentiles, "some Greeks" who had come to worship God at the Passover Feast told Philip that they would like the opportunity to see Jesus (John 12:20–21). The news triggered something deep within Jesus and He released words that wed death to life:

» "The hour has come for the Son of Man to be glorified." (John 12:23)
» "Unless a kernel of wheat falls to the ground and dies, it remains only a single seed. But if it dies, it produces many seeds." (John 12:24)
» "Anyone who loves their life will lose it, while anyone who hates their life in this world will keep it for eternal life." (John 12:25)
» "Whoever serves me must follow me; and where I am, my servant also will be. My Father will honor the one who serves me." (John 12:26)

Consider the progression of Jesus' statements: 1) It is time; 2) Death multiplies life; 3) If you hold life too tightly, you will lose it eternally; and 4) To love Me is to follow Me and, consequently, to be honored by the Father.

Jesus spoke to His disciples, and it also seems as though He spoke to Himself. His voice released—and His will responded to—timeless principles of life and truth. Then, in the hearing of His closest followers, Jesus said, "Now my soul [ψυχή (psychē)] is troubled [ταράσσω (tarassō)]" (John 12:27). He stated (aloud) that His "inner self, mind, thoughts, feelings, heart, and being"[1] were *tarasso*, which can mean to "stir up, cause great distress, trouble, disturb, cause a riot, throw into confusion."[2] In that moment, Jesus' self-described *psychē* resembled more of a stormy sea than a mild meadow.

Pause a moment to take in this reality: Jesus was troubled. Other than as an awkward (or perhaps even passive-aggressive) introduction to a personal or cultural rebuke, when was the last time you heard a leader confess, "My soul is troubled"? Yet, from Jesus' life, *holy can feel troubled.* Does it trouble us that Jesus felt troubled? Is Jesus' disclosure consistent with our images of Him? These are critical questions because they reveal the attitudes and actions we have associated with words like *holy, sinless,* and *sanctified* for Jesus, and, subsequently, for ourselves.

Jesus then followed up this somewhat startling statement by asking, "What shall I say? 'Father, save me from this hour'? No, it was for this very reason I came to this hour. Father, glorify your name!" (John 12:27–28). It had taken Jesus over thirty years to arrive at "this hour," and "this hour" was still far from over. Every step up to John 12 and every step after John 12 was a physical manifestation of His *psychē*'s commitment to glorify His Father's Name.[3]

Obedience is not a moment: it is a process connected by countless moments. Jesus neither started obeying nor finished obeying in John 12. Thanks to the Holy Spirit's inspiration and John's pen, what we witness in John 12 is a deeply significant (but not stand-alone) moment in Jesus'

> "No intellectual answer will solve suffering. Perhaps this is why God sent his own Son as one response to human pain, to experience it and absorb it into himself. The Incarnation did not 'solve' human suffering, but at least it was an active and personal response. In the truest sense, no words can speak more loudly than the Word."
>
> —PHILIP YANCEY[4]

journey of becoming "obedient to death—even death on a cross!" (Philippians 2:8).

And in the midst of Jesus' journey, He felt troubled. Clearly, then, a troubled soul is not always the sign of a faith deficit. A troubled soul is sometimes the signature of obedience-in-the-making. The obedience of Christ that set us free on the cross was the closing parenthesis on earth of a long process, not of a sudden decision. Likewise, when we hear Jesus' "Come, follow Me," our opening "Yes!" and the Father's closing "Well done!" are connected by countless moments in which we discern and reconfirm our decision to follow over and over and over again.

And, evidently, in the process, it is Christlike to on occasion blurt out, "My soul is troubled!"

Reflection

Remember a time in which your heart was troubled for a less-than-holy reason, such as fear of the future. Then contrast that feeling with a time where, like Jesus, your heart was troubled as obedience-in-the-making. Looking back, are you able to discern any differences between the two experiences? For me personally, in both situations I feel tension, but in the former I find myself processing alone in my head whereas in the latter, the tense conversation is with God. Investing time in discerning these differences can help us navigate them the next time God's will and our emotions are not in perfect sync.

Today's Fast: Premature Resolution

Process can be a troublesome thing. It disrupts us and disorients us and we would much rather skip to the end. But to live true, we must allow process to run its course. Question it, weep through it, agonize over it ... but, for the sake of our souls, we dare not truncate process because time alone makes its work soul-deep.

Today, fast premature resolution. Resist tidying up when you are in the muddy middle of the process of obedience-in-the-making. Befriend undone. Name the trouble. Like Jesus, talk to yourself and your Father God. Ask Him if alternative routes exist again and again and again ... until you push through resistance, pass around resentment, press past resignation, and emerge into willful (even if tearful) partnership with God.

On Lent

Fasting, part one. As mentioned yesterday, a dissertation could (and should) be devoted to exploring Lenten fasts. The practice of fasting has been politically, socially, and ecclesiastically laden with meaning since early times,[5] and a source of heated discussion between the Orthodox East and Roman Catholic West, as well as among the Reformers of the sixteenth century, many of whom equated fasting with yet another works-based deception.[6]

The days and length of the Lenten fast have varied from city to city and tradition to tradition. For example, in early times, believers in Jerusalem fasted over a period of eight weeks, totaling forty days exclusive of Saturday and Sunday. However, in Rome the fast lasted six weeks and included Saturdays.[7] Likewise, permissible foods varied, as evidenced by Pope St. Gregory's late sixth-century ruling that all should "abstain from flesh, meat, and all things that come from flesh, as milk, cheese, and eggs."[8] Some ate fish on designated days, some ate one meal a day, and the timing of breaking the fast—as well as how strictly the fast was enforced[9]—varied from era to era. The purpose of fasting was understood in many ways, including identification with the poor, an intentional journey into physical and spiritual brokenness,[10] a return to God,[11] "joy-creating sorrow,"[12] and the "withdrawing from sinful practices."[13]

Today's Reading: John 18:1–11

DAY TWENTY-TWO

A fter Jesus verbally reaffirmed His resolve to not ask for deliverance from "this hour," John records the following:

> [Jesus said] "Father, glorify your name!" Then a voice came from heaven, "I have glorified it, and will glorify it again." The crowd that was there and heard it said it had thundered; others said an angel had spoken to him. Jesus said, "This voice was for your benefit, not mine." (John 12:28–30)

Jesus was continually in conversation with His Father. Yet the Gospel writers only documented three times in which Father God's side of the conversation was broadcast publicly: at Jesus' baptism, at Jesus' transfiguration, and prior to the Last Supper. In all three instances,[1] Father's "voice" [φωνή (phōnē)] came from above in either a "cloud" [νεφέλη (nephelē)] or from "heaven" [οὐρανός (ouranos), the "abode of God"].[2]

Phōnē describes an audible sound. God's *sound*—imagine! At the Jordan River, it seems that only Jesus and perhaps John the Baptist[3] understood what God's sound said. At the Transfiguration, Peter, James, and John interpreted God's sound accurately but obeyed Jesus' instructions to tell no one until after His resurrection. And in John's gospel, prior to the Last Supper, listeners interpreted God's sound as thunder or an interaction between Jesus and an angel.

I would love to hear God's sound. My guess is that I am not alone. Perhaps you also ache to hear God say something audible. Why? About what? Our answers reveal our deepest longings and heartaches. Note how Father used His audible sound in the Gospels. At the baptism, instead of a pre-desert temptation motivational speech, Father used His sound to say, "You're My Son. I love you." At the Transfiguration, instead of expounding earth-shaking theological axioms, Father used His sound to tell the disciples to listen up, because "This is My Son. I love Him." Then before the Last Supper, Father publicly used His sound once more to respond to Jesus' troubled heart and firm resolve by saying, "I'll glorify My name again," or, if you will permit even more of a paraphrase, "I've heard your request. I'll do what I promised. Son, I won't let you down."

Hearing God's sounds from above would be remarkable, as those who have been graced with such experiences attest. But perhaps the reason Jesus said that the audible voice from Father "was for your benefit, not mine" (John 12:30) was because He lived in continuous attention to Father's inaudible voice. Like Jesus, we can attend to Father's sound within our spirits. As fruit of Jesus' resolve recorded in John 12, Father's voice reaches our very depths. Sometimes God's voice sounds like thunder, at other times like angels; almost always for me it sounds like silence as I open the Scriptures. Others' inability to hear it cannot invalidate it. Our inability to understand it cannot void it. God's *phōnē* sounds within His Son's followers, saying, "You are known. You are heard. You are loved. You are mine. I, your heavenly Father, keep My promises."

Reflection

Have you ever heard God's voice audibly? If so, recall the context and the content. What area of your life was God's *phōnē* comforting, convicting, or guiding? If you have not heard His audible voice, are you at peace with the silence? Have you ever wondered if there was "something wrong" blocking the way? Some church cultures are filled with testimonies of "what God spoke to me," and others would never dare to make such a claim. From the Scriptures, it would seem that audible sounds are far more rare than the inaudible (yet invaluable) way in which God continually speaks to us in our hearts.

Today's Fast: Sound

Today, attempt to fast sounds for an hour. Turn off your music, TV, and phone. Power down anything that beeps or buzzes or blinks. Then attend to your responses: Are you restless or restful without the filler? Is your mind more or less distractible? Is the aloneness comforting or unsettling? Ask God to reveal to you the power this world's sounds have in your life. Then ask Him to reveal to you the power His sounds have in your soul.

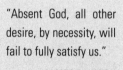
"Absent God, all other desire, by necessity, will fail to fully satisfy us."
—JAMES DAVISON HUNTER[4]

On Lent

Fasting, part two. One unifying theme in fasting is evident across the centuries and throughout all traditions: fasting is vain nonsense if understood and practiced only as abstinence from food. Consider a few of the numerous inspirational and quotable passages I encountered while researching fasting:

What then is fasting for us Christians? It is our entrance and participation in that experience of Christ Himself by which He liberates us from the total dependence on food, matter, and the world . . . All this means that deeply understood, fasting is the only means by which man recovers his true spiritual nature.[5]

(From *The Wednesday in the First Week Vespers*, Tone Eight) While fasting with the body, brethren, let us also fast in spirit. Let us loose every bond of iniquity; let us undo the knots of every contract made by violence; let us tear up all unjust agreements; let us give bread to the hungry and welcome to our house the poor who have no roof to cover them, that we may receive great mercy from Christ our God.[6]

(Citing *Homilies on Fasting*, I, 10 P.G. xxxi, 181B) It is useless to fast from food, protests St. Basil, and yet to indulge in cruel criticism and slander: "You do not eat meat, but you devour your brother."[7]

Today's Reading: John 18:12–14

_____

_____

_____

_____

_____

_____

_____

_____

DAY TWENTY-THREE

Though all the Gospels documented the Last Supper inclusive of Jesus' predictions of Judas's betrayal and Peter's denial, only John additionally included the oft-cited foot washing. Beautifully crafted sermons have helped us visualize the awkwardness of the scene: Jesus with a water basin and towel kneeling to wash disciples with dirty feet and hesitant hearts. We rightly consider this passage among the most poignant scriptural examples of servant leadership and have committed Jesus' explanation of His actions to memory: "Now that I, your Lord and Teacher, have washed your feet, you also should wash one another's feet. I have set you an example that you should do as I have done for you" (John 13:14–15).

"Why did Jesus do this?" we ask. "Because He was setting an example for us," we conclude confidently, correctly…and perhaps incompletely. Yes, without question Jesus exemplified servant leadership in the foot washing. But Jesus was (and is) more than a tutorial. Because we struggle to comprehend the incarnational reality of Jesus as fully God and fully man, we have a tendency to lean toward His divinity in reading the Gospels and, consequently, we interpret Jesus' actions as object lessons—sort of like a grief counselor who has never personally grieved because he or she is somehow smart enough to stay ahead of loss. Yet, as we have been reminded of in recent days, Jesus was familiar with grief and anger, just as we are.[1]

Jesus hinted at "more" of the story when Peter was inching away from the water basin: "You do not realize now what I am doing, but later you will understand" (John 13:7). Surely "later" was not code for "in a few minutes." Sometime in the future, the disciples would have more experience and more information with which to more deeply understand what Jesus was doing. So what did Jesus know then that the disciples would know only later? What information were they yet to receive that would cause them to revisit this experience with new insight? Many possibilities come to mind, but perhaps the most relevant are the following:

» At the table, Judas had thirty silver coins on him as payment for betraying Jesus.[2]
» At the table, Peter was unknowingly in such severe bondage to fear that it would soon incite him to "call down curses on himself" and to swear that he did not know Jesus.[3]
» At the table, the same disciples who would soon pledge to die with Christ would, shortly after, abandon Christ to save their own lives.[4]

At the table, Jesus washed the feet of a betrayer, a denier, and ten deserters. Pause to place yourself in this scene. Think of someone who has betrayed you, denied your love, or run away in your time of need. What would it take, what would it mean, for you to wash their feet? I obviously have never been in Jesus' position, but one personal experience helps me consider this familiar story anew.

Some of you may know that my husband and I have three children through the miracle of adoption, and that all three have mild to moderate special needs that sing delightful duets with special strengths. Our youngest's in utero drug exposure affected his ability to emotionally regulate. He is growing and healing, but in the not-too-distant past, little buddy would kick and say painful things (that I am glad he will not remember) when he became disregulated. Do you know what helped him in those moments? Foot massages. With coconut oil in hand, I would ask him if he would like a massage. Then, in a swerving, Jedi-like manner—to avoid any flailing fists—I applied gentle pressure to his gorgeous feet. It helped him. And it helped me. Honestly, I could actually feel love swelling and forgiveness expanding as I served my son in this way.

May I suggest that washing others' feet keeps us clean too? If so, perhaps Jesus was washing and forgiving and attending to His own heart simultaneously. Disciple after disciple, Jesus took their dirt and left them clean. And then one day most—though sadly not all—looked back and understood that with every rinse of the water and every pat of the towel, Jesus was saying, "I forgive you in advance for your upcoming epic fail. Though it will surprise you, remember that it does not surprise Me. My love will still be here when you return."

> "God's mercy is greater than our sins. There is an awareness of sin that does not lead to God but rather to self-preoccupation. Our temptation is to be so impressed by our sins and failings and so overwhelmed by our lack of generosity that we get stuck in a paralyzing guilt. It is the guilt that says: 'I am too sinful to deserve God's mercy.' It is the guilt that leads to introspection instead of directing our eyes to God. It is the guilt that has become an idol and therefore a form of pride. Lent is the time to break down this idol and to direct our attention to our Loving Lord."
>
> —HENRI NOUWEN (1932–1996)[5]

Reflection

In the foot washing, Jesus knelt before those who were deeply committed to Him. Even Judas, the only one who had strayed from that devotion, would—*prior* to Jesus' sentencing—return the silver coins to the rulers and confess, "'I have sinned,' he said, 'for I have betrayed innocent blood'"

(Matthew 27:4). I mention this because some sincere soul is going to contact me and ask if Jesus' example means that they should wash their spouse's feet whilst being used as a punching bag. Not based upon this text. Jesus did not take His water basin to the Praetorium to wash the feet of the soldiers who were about to flog Him. In context, Jesus washed the feet of loyal followers with hidden weaknesses that would soon surprise them. So in application, think of those who truly love you, but whose unrecognized weaknesses pain you. Prayerfully consider an act of strong servanthood that can wash their feet and keep your heart clean.

Today's Fast: Armchair Jesus

In case this image is not universal, allow me to explain. I am not a fan of football . . . or baseball or basketball, or really any sport other than golf. (Though I digress, this condition resulted in part from my abysmally low spatial intelligence that placed all team sports beyond my reach. But even apart from that, golf is a remarkably reasonable sport that involves the elements, your mind, serene spaces, and little sweat.) My dad, though a fan of all of the above, had no tolerance for watchers who were armchair coaches. Such individuals coach what they have never played. They give advice where they have never needed to take it. Dad found armchair coaches arrogant and annoying, and whether in sports or in life, many of us probably agree with him.

How wonderful for us all that Jesus is not an armchair coach. As Hebrews 4:15 affirms: "we do not have a high priest who is unable to sympathize with our weaknesses, but we have one who has been tempted in every way, just as we are—yet he did not sin." John states that, "In the beginning was the Word, and the Word was with God, and the Word was God. He was with God in the beginning" (John 1:1–2). Then John continues to unfold the mystery of the incarnation by adding, "The Word became flesh and made his dwelling among us" (John 1:14).

Today, I invite you to fast images of an Armchair Jesus. Such a perspective *of* Him hinders intimacy *with* Him. Jesus is not aloofly watching you. Jesus is always with you. He does not offer you hypothetical, armchair advice: Jesus offers you Himself. As with any relationship, sharing life is much easier when you believe you have shared ground.

On Lent

Fasting, part three. Today, we will continue our consideration of quotes on the subject of fasting.

God desires that his people cease their unjust practices, and their neglect of the poor and hungry. Depriving oneself of food is not necessarily laudable in God's eyes, but depriving others of food is indeed culpable. Tearing one's garments as a sign of repentance does not atone for failing to provide clothing to those who need it.[6]

(Citing Augustine, *Sermon 263*, FCS, vol. 38, 391–396) Hence, He fasted for forty days before the death of His Body as if to say, "abstain from the desires of this world." But He ate and drank during the forty days after the Resurrection of His Body, as if to say, "Behold I am with you . . . even to the end of the age."[7]

(Pope Francis, Ash Wednesday Mass) "Fasting makes sense if it really chips away at our security and, as a consequence, benefits someone else, if it helps us cultivate the style of the good Samaritan, who bent down to his brother in need and took care of him."[8]

Today's Reading: John 18:15–18

_____

_____

_____

_____

_____

_____

_____

_____

_____

_____

_____

_____

_____

DAY TWENTY-FOUR

During the Last Supper, after Jesus shocked Peter and the disciples with a prophecy about their soon-coming desertion, John's gospel preserved for future readers a magnificent compilation of Jesus' final teachings. Many years ago, I began to study a simple sentence within these chapters that held profound insight regarding the route and ultimate destination of Jesus' "Follow Me." In John 14:31, hidden between Jesus' messages about the coming of the Spirit and abiding in the vine, Jesus told His disciples, "Come now, let us leave," and proceeded to teach for another twenty minutes. In the Greek, the sentence is structured as a command [Ἐγείρεσθε (*Egeiresthe*) "Come"] followed by an exhortation [ἄγωμεν (*agōmen*) "let us leave"] and an adverb [ἐντεῦθεν (*enteuthen*) "from here"].

The command especially caught my interest. In various forms, *egeirō* occurs in Scripture more than 140 times, so I spent a few weeks (yes, in my ancient pre-Bible-study-software days) examining each occurrence to learn how the word was used specifically within the book of John and comparatively throughout the New Testament. *Egeirō* is an ordinary, as opposed to a deeply theological, word that appears in a small handful of contexts, all of which have in common the theme of *transition*. Most often, *egeirō* refers to the transition from death to life and is translated accordingly as *raised, raised to life, raised again, raised from the dead, rise,* or *risen.* In roughly a quarter of occurrences, *egeirō* is used to describe a transition of posture, most often in the context of the miraculous. This is how *egeirō* is used by Jesus when He said "Get up!" to the paralytic (Matthew 9:6), to Jairus's daughter (Mark 5:41), to the widow's dead son in Nain (Luke 7:14), and to the invalid at the pool of Bethesda (John 5:8).

However, in John 14:31 we encounter a usage of *egeirō* that reflects only 6 percent of all occurrences. *Egeirō,* as it appears in this simple sentence, has less to do with the miraculous than with the extraordinarily ordinary; less to do with life after death than with crucifixion during life. In John 14:31, *egeirō* refers to a transition in direction: it provides instructions for movement from a certain place in a specific direction.

Jesus' words were announcing a shift in His, and His disciples', story. In short, it was time to purposefully get moving. Personally, I translate John 14:31 as "Get up! Get going!"[1]—which begs the rather logical question of "Where?"

Where was it that Jesus wanted His disciples then—and, I suggest, His disciples today—to get up and get going toward?

Since you are already familiar with the rest of the story, I will skip to the destination and, over the next several days, describe the route. Where was Jesus headed? The cross. As we read in Luke 9:51, "As the time approached for him to be taken up to heaven, Jesus resolutely set out for Jerusalem." Note that Jesus did not start with this revelation. When calling the first disciples, Jesus said, "Follow Me" not "Follow Me to the cross."

The disciples, no doubt, started following Jesus with great respect and sincere admiration. However, love needs

> "There is no one-size-fits-all crucifixion. Jesus said each one of us must pick up our own cross, and pick it up each day. For some, martyrdom might be fame. For some, martyrdom might be anonymity. Regardless of what it is, first followers ask daily, 'Lord, what is my cross today, and where shall I carry it?'"
>
> —LEONARD SWEET[2]

time to grow before it has the strength to go wherever the Beloved beckons. Though all would stumble, one would bail, and none could fathom the cost, the disciples from John 14:31 forward followed Jesus cross-ward. Through the pain to come, Jesus fixed His gaze upon the truly great fruitfulness awaiting Him on the other side of truly great sacrifice. Cross-ward is a commitment that passion may make but that only love can keep.

Reflection

How would you describe the difference between passion and love? Think of your spiritual journey and consider the following: Has passion ever led you somewhere that love would not have gone? Has love ever led you somewhere that passion could not have gone?

Today's Fast: Neutrality

Cross-talk can be rather confusing. On the one hand, we are told that Jesus endured the cross so we would not have to, and to the extent that "the cross" means the "place of redemptive sacrifice," that is correct. Jesus died in our place to reconcile us to God (2 Corinthians 5:18). On the other hand, Jesus Himself told us to "take up [our] cross daily" (Luke 9:23);[3] therefore, when we define the cross as "self-denial," the fact that Jesus went through it does not mean that we get to go around it.

The disciples, too, were baffled by what *the cross* meant to Jesus. When Peter chided Jesus for His predictions of doom and gloom awaiting in Jerusalem, Jesus said,

> "Get behind me, Satan! You are a stumbling block to me; you do not have in mind the things of God, but merely human concerns." Then Jesus said to his disciples, "Whoever wants to be my disciple must

deny themselves and take up their crosses and follow me. For whoever wants to save their life will lose it, but whoever loses their life for me will find it. What good will it be for someone to gain the whole world, yet forfeit their soul?" (Matthew 16:23–26)[4]

"Deny" is translated from ἀπαρνέομαι (*aparneomai*), which means to "claim no knowledge or relationship to."[5] The word appears eleven times and, of interest, is also used by Jesus when telling Peter that he would disown Him three times (Matthew 26:34).

Deny self or deny Jesus: this is the crux. Remaining neutral is not an option. We have to choose a side. Today, fast neutrality. In the small, undocumented details of life, choose Jesus over self and recommit to living cross-ward.

The cross is the ultimate call to decrease. *The cross* is a call not to forget our own names but to live and die for the Name of Another. *The cross* is a call to renounce self-direction and shift leadership loyalties from our *selves* to our *Savior*.

On Lent

In the course of my study, I had the opportunity to interview Mark Bradshaw, who offered a well-researched and moving explanation of fasting from the perspective of his Orthodox tradition, an excerpt of which will be offered over the next three days. As you read, allow Mark's passion for Christ's resurrection to breathe fresh focus into your journey.

Bradshaw Interview, part one: "In the Orthodox Tradition, Lent, or the Great Fast, is about expectation and preparation. To fully understand what Lent means for the Orthodox, first you have to understand a bit about Orthodox Easter, known as Pascha (Passover), and the liturgical year. While many traditions have developed in such a way that Christmas becomes the main celebration of the year, for the Orthodox, Pascha is always the Feast of Feasts. The liturgical year is anchored by Pascha and all other movable feasts are measured by it. Pascha is preceded by a week of preparatory services known as Holy Week, in addition to the forty days of Lent, and three weeks of pre-Lenten services. All together there are about fifty days of fasting, balanced on the other side with fifty days of feasting until the time of Pentecost. Almost one-third of the year is bound up in the process of the celebration of Pascha for the Orthodox Christian."[6]

Today's Reading: John 18:19–24

_____

_____

_____

_____

_____

_____

_____

_____

_____

DAY TWENTY-FIVE

Imagine a time line with two points: John 14:31 ("Get up! Get going!") and the cross. Over the next week, we will connect these points via specific stops Jesus made in His journey cross-ward. In John 17, Jesus concluded the Last Supper with a three-part prayer for Himself, His disciples, and future believers. Then the group sang a hymn and "went out to the Mount of Olives . . . to a place called Gethsemane" (Matthew 26:30, 36), a name derived from the Hebrew *gath schmanim*, which means "oil presses."[1] John further described the place as a κῆπος (*kēpos*), which is most often translated "garden."[2] The exact coordinates of the garden today are a matter of conjecture, but in Jesus' day, the Mount of Olives was graced with thick groves that, by Josephus's records, were cut down by Titus in the AD 70 siege on Jerusalem.[3] There, in a garden that had so often been a place of comfort and refuge,[4] we read that Jesus "began to be sorrowful and troubled. Then he said to them, 'My soul [ψυχή (*psychē*)] is overwhelmed with sorrow to the point of death. Stay here and keep watch with me'" (Matthew 26:37–38).

Stop #1: Overwhelming Sorrow. Get up and get going where? Into a preparatory period of grieving. Consider the weight of Jesus' word choice. "To be sorrowful" was translated from λυπέομαι (*lypeomai*), which speaks of "grief, distress, vex, and pain." "Troubled" was chosen to reflect ἀδημονέω (adēmoneō), which means to "be in anxiety" or "distressed." "Overwhelmed with sorrow" was selected to capture περίλυπος (perilypos), which means, "deeply grieved." And "death," θάνατος (thanatos), was also translated as "plague" in Revelation 6:8.[5] Luke added further vivid detail to Jesus' distress in Gethsemane: "An angel from heaven appeared to him and strengthened him. And being in anguish, he prayed more earnestly, and his sweat was like drops of blood falling to the ground" (Luke 22:43–44).

Only Jesus, the Father, and the Holy Spirit understood the unspeakable cost Jesus would pay for our sins to be forgiven. Under the crushing weight of all that was to come, Jesus offered variations of the same prayer three times: "My Father, if it is possible, may this cup be taken from me. Yet not as I will, but as you will'" (Matthew 26:39, 42, 44). We rightly hear this as the ultimate manifestation of Christ's submission to the Father, but there is also within Jesus' prayer a theological question that is extremely relevant today: *Is there another way? If so, I want to take it.*

Within our global culture, it sounds enlightened and egalitarian to believe in many ways to God, which makes wrestling with this text all the more critical. Is there another way for mankind to be reconciled to God? Here in the Garden of Gethsemane, Jesus pressed Father with this very question three times: "My Father, if it is possible, may this cup be taken from me." Clearly, by the events that follow, Father's answer was "no": another way did not exist. Jesus was and is "The Way" (John 14:6). As Jesus continued cross-ward, He took each sorrowful step certain that His death and resurrection were the only way to the Father for us. The price was astounding, but Jesus loved us enough to pay it.

Sharing Jesus' certainty honors Jesus' sacrifice.[6]

> "What matters is *participating in the reality of God and the world in Jesus Christ today*, and in doing so in such a way that I never experience the reality of God without the reality of the world, nor the reality of the world without the reality of God."
>
> —DIETRICH BONHOEFFER (1906–1945)[7]

Reflection

What cup would you rather not drink? Today find a quiet corner to follow Jesus' example. Offer up Jesus' prayer: "My Father, if it is possible, may this cup be taken from me. Yet not as I will, but as You will." Then sit in silence with your journal nearby.

Today's Fast: Denial

Note that Jesus did not try to deny His emotions in the garden but instead expressed them honestly, respectfully, and repeatedly: He pleaded with Father three times for "this cup" to pass. Honesty is a friend of intimacy with God and, conversely, denial is an enemy of intimacy with God. As Larry S. Julian stated, "Hiding who you are . . . isn't the solution."[8]

From Jesus' example, it is clear that a misalignment between our desires and God's will is not sin. Jesus was victorious not because He lacked uncooperative feelings but because He affirmed and reaffirmed His commitment to honor Father's will above His emotions.

Today, fast denial. Be honest with yourself so that you can be honest with God. In Jesus' prayer, He did not deny His emotions but rather ushered them to their safest position: behind His will.[9]

On Lent

Bradshaw Interview, part two: "Of course most people are aware of Lent because of the fast. The Orthodox fast during Lent is basically a vegan diet. Almost all animal products are eliminated from the diet, including meat and dairy, as well as olive oil and wine. On the weekends the fast relaxes a little, and oil and wine are allowed again. One notable difference between Orthodox and Roman Catholic observances of Lent is the common Catholic practice of choosing something to give up for Lent, rather than having a communal fast. The Orthodox church maintains the ancient fasting practices, and does not have a place for individualized fasting. Fasting, like almost all sacred and ascetic practices in Orthodoxy, is communal in nature. We are saved in community, as the Body of Christ, and so our ascetic endeavors reflect this. We practice unity among the believers by engaging in the struggle of Lent together, fasting in the same way and at the same time.

"Fasting shouldn't be viewed as an oppressive action of the many against the individual. While the struggle is something for the entire community, fasting in Orthodoxy is never engaged in as a duty. Fasting is an ascetic practice, meaning it is viewed as spiritual training, much in the same way that lifting weights or running would be for the body. Every chance to fast has a multitude of spiritual benefits, but is not a burden against Christ's law of grace. You do not incur a sin guilt or debt by not fasting, but you miss out on a sweet gift of the Holy Spirit to the church that is meant for your inner health."[10]

Today's Reading: John 18:25–27

_____

_____

_____

_____

_____

_____

DAY TWENTY-SIX

The image of Jesus agonizing in prayer, surrounded by ancient trees that He watered with His weeping, moves me profoundly. In the beginning of His public ministry, Jesus' temptation took place in a desert. Toward the end of His public ministry, His cross-ward travail was hosted in a garden. In the desert, Jesus was alone with the exception of wild animals and attending angels. In the garden, angels returned to strengthen Jesus while His disciples slept a few yards away. Something deep within me aches over Jesus' aloneness in this space.

He did not want to be *that* alone.

Eleven disciples had followed Jesus into the garden that night. Jesus told eight, "Sit here while I go over there and pray" (Matthew 26:36). Then, reminiscent of—but not remotely a repeat of—the Transfiguration, Jesus selected Peter, James, and John to go further into the garden. Why? Jesus stated, "Stay here and keep watch with me" (Matthew 26:38). "Keep watch" is translated from γρηγορέω (*grēgoreō*), which can mean, "to stay awake," "be alert," or "be vigilant."[1] Jesus requested His disciples' active support. In that garden, more than in any prior moment of their journey together, Jesus asked His disciples to rise up and serve Him as prayerful "watchmen on the walls" (Isaiah 62:6).

Two layers of disciples were now between Jesus and the soon-coming, club-wielding crowd. As Jesus found a solitary place, fell to the ground, and prayed, His nearest support group fell asleep because "their eyes were heavy" (Matthew 26:43). Luke explained that the disciples' slumber was neither laziness nor lovelessness. The trio was simply "exhausted from sorrow" (Luke 22:45). Unbeknownst to the disciples, the Last Supper had ush-

> "There are two absences of God. One is the absence that condemns us, the other is the absence that sanctifies us. In the absence that is condemnation, God 'knows us not' because we have put some other god in His place, and refuse to be known by Him. In the absence that sanctifies, God empties the soul of every image that might become an idol and of every concern that might stand between our face and His."
>
> —THOMAS MERTON (1915–1968)[2]

ered them into the most disillusioning days of their walk with Jesus. His "Follow Me" had not led to any scenario they had envisioned. Jesus' cross-talk confused them, the escalating animosity from the religious leadership alarmed them, and now Jesus Himself confessed that He was overwhelmed by sorrow. No wonder they closed their eyes!

If you have ever been exhausted from sorrow, you probably can empathize with the disciples. Summoning the will to keep watch in such seasons is strenuous. Sometimes I, like the disciples, have defaulted to my pillow instead of to prayer in the denial-laden hope that somehow all would be set right again when I opened my eyes.

In between all three agonizing sets of prayer, Jesus returned to find His watchmen unwatchful. He chose to wake them only once. When He did, it was clear to Peter, James, and John that Jesus' sorrow had not lifted. Still troubled in soul, Jesus once again asked His disciples for their alert presence:

> "Couldn't you men keep watch with me for one hour?" he asked Peter. "Watch and pray so that you will not fall into temptation. The spirit [πνεῦμα (pneuma)] is willing, but the flesh [σάρξ (sarx)] is weak." (Matthew 26:40–41)

When discouraged, we are far more vulnerable to deception. In their disillusioned state, Peter, James, and John received a strong word from Jesus: "Watch and pray for your sake and for Mine." Hindering their hearing in the garden, however, was a heaviness that defied description: something was growing in the shadows.[3] Later, Jesus would name it: this was the hour "when darkness reigns" (Luke 22:53). Before the growing darkness overtook them, Jesus, in agony, did in the garden what His disciples would only much later have the strength to emulate: Jesus watched and prayed His way cross-ward.

Reflection

"He did not want to be *that* alone." Jesus requested the disciples' companionship: their alert presence could have been a comfort to Him. We know that Jesus' presence is valuable to us, but we rarely consider the possibility that our presence is valuable to Him. Today, reflect upon this concept of Jesus treasuring your companionship.

Today's Fast: Comparison

We have considered the three, now let us consider the eight. Picture Jesus leaving them closer to the garden entrance and taking the three (once again) further in with Him. The eight had seen this before. Last time the three came back with faces aglow and obviously "in the know" about some wonder they could not share.

Now here they were again, separated from the three. Knowing that comparison was a frequent struggle among the disciples, how might they have felt? How have you felt when others seem closer to a leader or even to God?

Today, fast comparison. Cease determining the value of your reality by your perceptions of others' reality. Bless and pray specifically for those who appear "closer in." (They may be overwhelmed with sorrow.)

On Lent

Bradshaw Interview, part three: "A spiritual father encouraged me to enter in very slowly, and not to take on too heavy of a burden. This proved to be excellent advice, as you can easily become overly legalistic in your fasting. Another piece of advice he gave was, 'Never look at another person's plate.' Your fast is your own, and you carry what you can bear. St John Chrysostom consoled everyone that no matter how much of the Lenten burden they were able to carry, God accepts it all, both the deed and the intention, with honors.[4]

"I said at the beginning that Lent is about preparation and expectation. What we prepare for, and what we expect, is the risen Lord 'trampling down death, by death.' Lent is a beautiful invitation for us to travel with the Lord into Jerusalem, to once again live out our baptism where we have been baptized into Christ's death (Romans 6:3), go with him through that experience and rise with him once again into the new life of the church. To try to experience the magnificence of Holy Week and the resurrection we go through the fast, purging our body and spirit of distractions, and preparing our hearts to go with Christ. In my experience that preparation makes the celebratory feast so much grander."[5]

Today's Reading: John 18:28–32

_____

_____

_____

_____

_____

_____

_____

_____

_____

_____

_____

_____

_____

DAY TWENTY-SEVEN

After committing for the third time in prayer to drink the cup if no other way existed for it to be emptied, Jesus returned to His disciples and said,

> Are you still sleeping and resting? Look, the hour is near, and the Son of Man is delivered into the hands of sinners. Rise! Let us go! Here comes my betrayer! (Matthew 26:45–46)

"Rise, let us go!"—they had heard this before. In the Greek, the phrase was Ἐγείρεσθε (*Egeiresthe*) ἄγωμεν (*agōmen*). This was a repeat of John 14:31: Get up and get going! Where?

Stop #2: A Coworker's Betrayal. Judas had not gone with the Eleven to the garden that night, but he was present for the Last Supper. Matthew, an eyewitness, recorded the interaction between Jesus and Judas at the dinner table. After Jesus told the disciples that one among them would betray Him, Judas said, "Surely you don't mean me, Rabbi?" To which Jesus replied, "You have said so" (Matthew 26:21, 25). Immediately following this exchange, Jesus broke the bread, called it His body, and offered it to the

Twelve. And Judas ate it. Then Jesus blessed the cup, called it the "blood of the covenant, which is poured out for many for the forgiveness of sins" (Matthew 26:28), and passed it to the Twelve. And Judas drank from it.

John, another eyewitness, adds, "As soon as Judas took the bread, Satan entered into him" (John 13:27). Judas had made his deal with the chief priests *before* the Last Supper: it was his own choice. But as Judas led the crowds with their clubs and the soldiers with their swords into the garden, internally he was no longer acting alone: this betrayal was a manifestation of satanic opposition.

We expect satanic opposition from the world. But when it comes from around the table, it takes our breath away. For three years, Judas and Jesus walked, talked, and served together. For three years, the Eleven trusted Judas with the moneybag. Judas saw the same miracles and received the same authority. Judas ate the same bread and drank from the same cup. And now, Judas kissed the King with blood money in his hands.

In considering this moment, we must resist any tendencies to make Jesus a stoic. Yes, Jesus saw it coming, but knowledge does not numb the soul to pain. Picture Jesus spending hours alone in gut-wrenching prayer, taking breaks only to discover His support team spiritually missing-in-action. Then,

> Judas, one of the Twelve, arrived. With him was a large crowd armed with swords and clubs, sent from the chief priests and the elders of the people. Now the betrayer had arranged a signal with them: "The one I kiss is the man: arrest him." Going at once to Jesus, Judas said, "Greetings, Rabbi!" and kissed him. Jesus replied, "Do what you came for, friend." (Matthew 26:47–50)

Betrayal of this degree is a toxic mixture of rejection, disregard, and narcissism. A betrayer sacrifices someone else for their own gain. As a result, many who have been betrayed experience anger, a sense of worthlessness, self-doubt, and soul-deep pain. Though Scripture does not disclose Jesus' emotions as He looked into Judas's eyes, we do know with confidence that Jesus understands betrayal.

Jesus and Judas's final interaction ended with some name-calling. The last name Judas called Jesus was *Rabbi*. The last thing Jesus called Judas was *friend*. The Greek ἑταῖρος (*hetairos*) was used culturally to refer to a colleague, comrade, fellow worker, or friend. It appears only three times in the New Testament, exclusively in the gospel of Matthew.[1] In biblical context, "the implication [is] of a distinct relationship in which there is generosity on the one part and abuse of it on the other."[2] To the point: a co-worker's betrayal.

> "If every annoyance can be made to remind me to turn and grip Your hand and ask You, 'What are you saying through this vexation?' then I can turn life's rough spots into Your vocabulary. If I can do that perfectly, nothing can defeat my soul."
>
> —FRANK LAUBACH
> (1884–1970)[3]

Reflection

Judas's story is a sad one. Some have suggested that he lacked the option of writing a different ending: that he was born a betrayer. Respectfully, I disagree and remain in that messy place theologically where God's sovereignty and human free will co-exist.

Think of those who once ate at the church's table and then somehow formed an alliance with darkness. What factors may have contributed to their departure? Pray for them, that unlike Judas, they will find their way back home.

Today's Fast: Discontentment

Judas held the moneybag, the power, and the honored position of being counted among the Twelve. Jesus in no way excluded him from ministry or shared authority. Yet somehow it was not enough. Judas obviously wanted more or something else or both. His sense of not having enough led him to steal from the moneybag (John 12:6) and fill his personal wallet with thirty silver coins. Even then, he still was not satisfied and tried to rewind his actions to no avail. It is as though Judas was plagued with a nagging sense of not-enough-ness.

One of the fiercest allies of not-enough-ness is our imaginations. Today, fast daydreaming of "more." Refuse to allow discontentment brain space. Each time you are tempted to picture your life with something else or something new or something different, stop. (Yes, I just said STOP.) And redirect your mental energy to thank God for anything in your current reality for which you can be grateful.

On Lent

Almsgiving. Considered part of a "triad" along with prayer and fasting,[4] almsgiving and fasting are from ancient times inextricable:

> The second-century *Shepherd of Hermas* insists that the money saved through fasting is to be given to the widow, the orphan and the poor (Similitudes, V, iii, 7). But almsgiving means more than this. It is to give not only our money but our time, not only what we *have* but what we *are*; it is to give a part of ourselves.[5]

In my research, I had the opportunity to interview a local Catholic priest esteemed as a historian. Fr. Lewis defined Lent as,

> A time of identifying more closely with the poor. That is where the almsgiving comes in. Almsgiving is not tithing . . . it doesn't hurt any of us to give something up. Whether it's giving up our cigarettes—I

don't smoke so that wouldn't be a hardship—I don't drink beer except very, very occasionally so that wouldn't be a hardship. But I love ice-cream. Okay, so if I give up ice-cream, I don't keep that money but I kind of calculate: "How much do I normally spend a week on ice-cream?" I give that as an alms to the poor.[6]

Personally, I found this marriage of almsgiving and abstinence inspiring because it connects personal decrease with community by designating generosity as the intended outcome of fasting.

Today's Reading: John 18:33–40

_____

_____

_____

_____

_____

_____

_____

_____

_____

DAY TWENTY-EIGHT

John's account of what happened after Judas's kiss is stunning. Jesus asked the crowd who they were looking for and they replied, "Jesus of Nazareth." When Jesus responded, "I am he," John documents that "they drew back and fell to the ground" (John 18:6). When they recovered, Jesus repeated the question and they replied with the same answer (though perhaps with a bit more hesitancy in their voices). This time, the One whose "I am he" had leveled a mob used His voice to shield His suddenly awake disciples: "If you are looking for me, then let these men go" (John 18:8).

Peter had no intentions of being "let go" at all, let alone without a fight. Drawing a sword, he whacked off the high priest's servant's ear. Then Jesus healed Malchus (the man who had come to arrest Him) and rebuked Peter (the man who had risked defending Him):

> Put your sword away! Shall I not drink the cup the Father has given me? (John 18:11)
>
> Do you think I cannot call on my Father, and he will at once put at my disposal more than twelve legions of angels? But how then would the Scriptures be fulfilled that say it must happen in this way? (Matthew 26:53–54)

The whole exchange was simply too upside-down for the Eleven. When the soldiers stepped forward to arrest and bind Jesus, the disciples "deserted Him and fled" (Matthew 26:56).

Stop #3: Voluntarily Restricted Freedom. The church is both afflicted and exhausted by the dizzying notion that God-given power should be exercised in every God-given-moment. Jesus makes it clear, however, that "can ≠ should."[1] Jesus' voice flattened armed soldiers, yet He permitted these self-declared enemies to stand up again. Jesus had angels at His disposal, yet declined to dispatch them. We dare not mistake these choices for passivity, resignation, or weakness. This dimension of strength was the fruit of power fully submitted to love. Elsewhere, I refer to this strength as the Discipline of Restraint:

> "To love righteousness is to make it grow, not to avenge it . . . Throughout His life on earth, He resisted every impulse to work more rapidly for a lower good."
>
> —GEORGE MACDONALD
> (1824–1905)[2]

Though a cousin of humility, the *Discipline of Restraint* is not related to *timidity*. Though a friend of patience, the *Discipline of Restraint* is not a form of *hesitation*.

Timidity is fear-driven.

Hesitation is doubt-driven.

Restraint is obedience-inspired.[3]

Jesus voluntarily accepted restricted freedom on the way cross-ward. Why? Because of His commitment to "this hour"[4] and "this cup."[5] In other hours Jesus turned over the tables of money changers. With other cups, He turned water into wine.[6] But this cup of suffering and this hour of darkness were a different matter. Jesus had committed to His Father to live them to the last drop. Surely, no amount of gifting could endure such a day. Only love could lead the way.

And so soldiers (who moments earlier had been toppled by three words) walked past Malchus (who moments earlier had his ear severed by a sword) and bound the healing hands of Jesus. The crowds thought themselves the victors as they led their prisoner out of the garden. In truth, prisoners were escorting the Victor to a triumph that would shake the gates of hell.

Reflection

A long time ago, a fitness trainer taught me that muscles grow through cycles of exercise and rest—not by constant use. In the same way, the gifts and strengths God has entrusted to us grow by cycles of exercising them and resting them. Resting is also a form of discipline. Jesus did not suddenly summon the strength to withhold His power from flattening the crowds permanently. Throughout His life, He displayed remarkable discipline in the use of His giftings and power. Today, think about your greatest strengths and consider how frequently you rest them.

Today's Fast: Formulas

In the density of real life, we can easily default to "always" or "never" formulas. My eldest, who is graced with the strengths of Asperger Syndrome (i.e., he is literal), pressed out of me any false confidence I might have had in formulas many years ago. "Jona, always listen to your teachers," I began. Without any rebellion in his heart, he asked, "Mom, even if they tell me there is no God?" "Uh, well not then..."

In the same way, Jesus resists our attempts to formulize Him. With reference to our focus today, Jesus did not *always* allow others to restrict His freedom. In direct defiance of the ruling elite, Jesus kept healing on Sabbaths and teaching on mountainsides and rebuking hypocrites. Up until the arrest, Jesus did not allow His voice or His body to be chained. For example, when He was rejected in Nazareth, the crowds tried to throw Him over a cliff and "he walked right through the crowd and went on his way" (Luke 4:30).

Likewise, after Jesus' ascension, the apostles did not always acquiesce to rulers' attempts to restrict their freedom. When commanded by the Sanhedrin not to "speak or teach at all in the name of Jesus," Peter and John replied, "Which is right in God's eyes: to listen to you, or to him? You be the judges!" (Acts 4:18–19). In other words, "No." Paul, as well, often transitioned to a different city when faced with life-threatening situations, but when God told him that he "must also testify in Rome" (Acts 23:11), he chose to restrict his freedom by appealing to Caesar instead of being set free (Acts 26:32). Evidently God's path in each instance of potentially restricted freedom seems to be found only in prayerful discernment.

Restricted freedom can come in a wide variety of forms: physical limitations, emotional challenges, dysfunction in those near us, decisions of those over us, laws that limit religious freedom, and economic downturns that affect our budgets and seem to threaten our dreams. Today, consider the restrictions you are experiencing—whether from disease, dysfunction, requirements, or rules. Fast formulas and instead spend time in prayerful discernment asking God to show you His way.

On Lent

Abstinence, part one. Though the word can be somewhat charged today, historically *abstinence* has been defined as, "The practice or discipline of resisting self-indulgence; self-restraint."[7] French missionary and priest John Eudes (1601–1680) is quoted as saying that "Abstinence is the mother of health. A few ounces of privation will prove an excellent recipe for any ailment."[8] It seems, however, that few have rushed out to make a T-shirt of Eudes's quote.

Indulgence is heralded in our day as a form of self-therapy. In truth, it has been heralded in every day but in forms we may find less familiar.

For example, theaters, horse racing, and public games were strongly discouraged in past centuries during Lent. For many spiritual leaders, there was an inherent dissonance between the sobriety of the Lenten season and the temporal glitter of public entertainment. An excellent, albeit rather dramatic, example of this prohibition is preserved in a Lenten sermon rebuke from Archbishop of Constantinople St. John Chrysostom (AD 347–407):

> When I consider, how at one blast of the devil ye have forgotten all my daily admonitions, and continued discourses, and run to that pomp of Satan, the horse race in the Circus; with what heart can I think of preaching to you again who have so soon let slip all that I said before? This is what chiefly raises my grief, yea, my anger and indignation, that together with my admonition ye have cast the reverence of this holy season of Lent out of your souls, and thrown yourselves into the nets of the devil.[9]

Today's Reading: John 19:1–6

_____

_____

_____

_____

_____

_____

As "this hour" of darkness lengthened, a bound Jesus was taken under guard from Annas[1] to Caiaphas[2] to Pilate[3] to Herod[4] and back to Pilate.[5] Much has been written about the judicial process that played out during Jesus' trials, as well as the motivations of all involved. Though I find both scholarly and speculative discussions intriguing (albeit somewhat inconclusive), I am drawn to Jesus in the center of the drama. How did He feel when Herod wanted Him to perform tricks like a circus animal? What was He thinking when Caiaphas tore his clothes and cried, "Blasphemy!" What motivated Him to speak to Annas and to be silent before Herod?

During the trials, Jesus was brought before two religious leaders (Annas and Caiaphas) and two military leaders (Pilate and Herod). The former accused Jesus of crimes against God, and then, once they had agreed on a charge of blasphemy, they brought Jesus to Pilate and accused Him of crimes against the state. Only eight of all the accusations levied against Jesus during the trials made it into the Gospels: two when Jesus stood before Caiaphas and the rest when Jesus stood before Pilate. Consider the veracity of the charges against Jesus listed chronologically below:

1. Claiming to be "able to destroy the temple of God and rebuild it in three days"[6] (Matthew 26:61).[7]
2. Speaking "blasphemy" because He believed Himself to be "the Messiah, the Son of God" (Matthew 26:63–66).[8]
3. Subverting the nation (Luke 23:2).
4. Opposing paying taxes to Caesar[9] (Luke 23:2).
5. Claiming "to be Messiah, a king"[10] (Luke 23:2).
6. Stirring "up the people all over Judea by his teaching" (Luke 23:5).
7. Claiming to be the "Son of God" (John 19:7).
8. As a self-acclaimed king, opposing Caesar[11] (John 19:12).

Get up and get going where?

Stop #4: Misrepresentation. During the trials, Jesus' words were manipulated, His faith doubted, and His character slandered. And of all the leaders involved, Pilate was the one who did not buy it. If the Gospels were the only account of Pilate's life, we might conclude that he was a spiritually discerning, and even moral, soul. However, Philo (25 BC–AD 50) described Pilate as a "man of a very inflexible disposition, and very merciless as well as very obstinate" who was no friend of the Jews.[12] Clearly, something about Jesus unnerved Pilate. He simply was not himself in Jesus' presence. Their last exchange was revealing: it captured how deeply unsettled Pilate felt about Jesus as well as Jesus' source of calm in the midst of misrepresentation:

> "The final step on the way to holiness in Christ is then to completely abandon ourselves with confident joy to the apparent madness of the cross."
>
> —THOMAS MERTON
> (1915–1968)[13]

The Jewish leaders insisted, "We have a law, and according to that law he must die, because he claimed to be the Son of God." When Pilate heard this, he was even more afraid, and he went back inside the palace. "Where do you come from?" he asked Jesus, but Jesus gave him no answer. "Do you refuse to speak to me?" Pilate said. "Don't you realize I have power either to free you or to crucify you?" Jesus answered, "You would have no power over me if it were not given to you from above." (John 19:7–11)

Jesus knew that man was neither the author nor the director of His life. He was certain that His future did not rest in the frail, fickle, fragile hands of human favor.

Consequently, *Jesus had no fear for Pilate to exploit.*

Jesus did not fear death. Jesus did not fear suffering. He possessed an authority that could be neither bought nor beaten: an interior authority that others could misrepresent but never intimidate.

Reflection

Matthew recorded that Pilate "knew it was out of envy [φθόνος (*phthonos*) envy, jealousy, self-interest] that they had handed Jesus over to him" (Matthew 27:18). Perhaps all of us have in our memories a time in which our reputation was stained by someone else's jealousy. Today, risk asking God to reveal if someone's reputation is currently being stained by yours.

Today's Fast: Intimidation

In this interaction between Jesus and Pilate, visible political power collided with invisible spiritual authority. Pilate attempted to intimidate Jesus with his position and Jesus entirely unnerved Pilate by His presence. In the reading, I noted that, "Jesus had no fear for Pilate to exploit." Fear is intimidation's oxygen. Skilled intimidators sniff out fear and then customize if-then strategies to compel compliance. Satan is a skilled intimidator. Wisdom invites us to discern where we are most vulnerable to his tactics.

What do you fear? Being misunderstood or misrepresented? Being unwanted or unneeded? Illness or injury? Today, seek to fast intimidation by not letting fear bully you. When you realize fear is being used to intimidate you, pause and verbalize this simple prayer: *Jesus, you have already embraced everything that I fear. I renounce fear's hold on me. By God's grace I share Your victory.* Will fear vaporize as you say "amen"? That would be lovely. But even more powerful is the fact that the cycle of awareness, resistance, and prayer decreases your vulnerability to intimidation by strengthening your will with Truth.

On Lent

Abstinence, part two. As I have informally observed the growing interest in Lent among my colleagues and friends, abstaining from public entertainment is among the most common Lenten commitments. However, this commitment manifests not in avoiding fairs and sporting events as much as it manifests in the realm of fasting social media. Frequently, as Lent begins, posts appear on social media sites alerting "friends" that a forty-day fast from social media is commencing. Whereas St. Chrysostom expresses concern over the "nets of the devil" cast by public entertainment, modern abstinence from public entertainment seems less motivated by avoiding sin and more inspired by both a longing to unplug and a concern that perhaps our souls have become addicted to (but unsatisfied by) online interaction.

Today's Reading: John 19:7–16

_____

_____

_____

_____

_____

_____

_____

_____

_____

_____

_____

_____

_____

DAY THIRTY

Interspersed between the accounts of Jesus' trials is the painful account of Peter's denial.[1] We know it well, and (if you are like me) wince each time the rooster crows. Somehow Peter's story affects us differently than does the story of Judas. Judas schemed against Jesus in secret. Peter tried to defend Jesus in public. Judas received compensation for his betrayal with thirty silver coins. Peter pledged to pay for his loyalty with his life. Judas intentionally deceived others. But Peter was unknowingly deceived about himself. Examining the accounts, I cannot question the authenticity of Peter's allegiance to Jesus. Sometimes fault lines can only be identified and mapped *after* an earthquake.

This is a sobering reality. We prefer our self-revelations pre-earthquake, thank you. However, some forms of disillusionment (such as Peter's loss of illusions about the strength of his commitment to Christ) can only be triggered by rather massive movements in the ground beneath our feet. Though we know this in our heads, it is shocking to discover it in our lives: there is more weakness within us than we can see. Further, there is more weakness within us than Jesus chooses to reveal to us. Frankly, we could not handle seeing everything Jesus sees.

Get up and going where?

Stop #5: A Friend's Failure. Looking into Peter's eyes at the Last Supper, Jesus discerned that His friend was both sincere *and* sincerely wrong about the depth of his devotion:

> Simon, Simon, Satan has asked to sift you as wheat. But I have prayed for you, Simon, that your faith may not fail.... I tell you, Peter, before the rooster crows today, you will deny three times that you know me. (Luke 22:31–32, 34)

Jesus knew Peter better than Peter knew himself. After Jesus' arrest, as fear placed a chokehold on Peter's love, Peter regressed to a state of sheer self-preservation: fight, flight, or freeze. He tried to fight and was told to put his sword away.[2] He then resorted to flight but returned to the court-yard of the high priest, anxious to learn more of Jesus' fate.[3] Then when those around the campfire called him out as a disciple of Jesus, Peter froze, denied all knowledge of Jesus,[4] and:

> Just as he was speaking, the rooster crowed. The Lord turned and looked straight at Peter. Then Peter remembered the word the Lord had spoken to him: "Before the rooster crows today, you will dis-own me three times." And he went outside and wept bitterly. (Luke 22:60–62)

Peter wept because Peter loved. Peter's illusion was not that he loved Jesus. Peter's illusion was that he loved Jesus more than he loved his own life.

As with Judas, Jesus saw it coming. As with Judas, Jesus felt it deeply. But He clearly prepared Peter differently for the soon-coming earth-quake. Whereas Judas was told, "What you are about to do, do quickly" (John 13:27),[5] Peter was told, "When you have turned back, strengthen your brothers" (Luke 22:32). Willfully deceiving and being deceived have

> "The triumph of grace is that we accept the humiliation of failure, which is indeed a triumph, a greater triumph than external success. In actual fact, the experience of failure in ministry teaches us in the long run how to do it, which is with complete dependence on God."
>
> —THOMAS KEATING[6]

different roots: the first is rebellion and the second is humanity. To quote King David (who knew what it was like to be disillusioned with himself): "As a father has compassion on his children, so the LORD has compassion on those who fear him; for he knows how we are formed, he remembers that we are dust" (Psalm 103:13–14).

So when an earthquake reveals internal fault lines that we never knew existed, and as the ground shakes we fall into our own disillusionment, we need to remember to get back up, receive forgiveness, and call upon our newly acquired humility to strengthen others.

Reflection

Be attentive today to God's conviction regarding any way in which you are willfully deceiving others or yourself. If He shows you an area to attend to, be encouraged: God does not reveal sin or weakness to mock us. God "reveals to heal."[7]

Today's Fast: Self-Confidence

Please, hear me out before you close the book. Yes, I know "self-confidence" is a highly valued attribute. But when it comes to our hearts, God-confidence is our only hope. Self is a poor discerner of self, whether or not it is confident. God searches our hearts and minds and His faithfulness is worthy of our trust. This surely is where David invested his hope when he prayed, "Search me, God, and know my heart; test me and know my anxious thoughts. See if there is any offensive way in me, and lead me in the way everlasting" (Psalm 139:23–24).

Peter could not see his fault line. But Jesus did. In the same way, we do not fully know our hearts. But Jesus does. Today, fast self-confidence and rest deeply in Jesus' promise that the Holy Spirit will "guide you into all the truth" (John 16:13).

On Lent

Abstinence, part three. Two other forms of abstinence appeared only in Orthodox literature: chastity[8] and the scheduling of festivities. Then Dean of St. Vladimir's Seminary, Fr. Thomas Hopko, explained that in the original language, *chastity*

> Is a combination of the word for wholeness and integrity, and the word for wisdom and understanding. This basically is what chastity is: soundness and wholeness, completeness and sanity. It is not something physical or biological. It is not something negative. . . . It is a spiritual condition. . . . There is an obsession with sexuality in our time. We have come to idolize sexual activity. We virtually enthrone it in the place of God in our lives.[9]

The stated intention of this form of fasting is the encouragement of spiritual intimacy in marriage and sexual self-control in the life of believers. Additionally, in some Orthodox communities, spiritual and private celebrations—inclusive of religious festivals and ceremonies—are fasted during Lent:[10]

> In the Christian Empire of Byzantium, theatres were closed and public spectacles forbidden during Lent; and even today weddings are forbidden in the seven weeks of the fast. Yet these elements of

austerity should not blind us to the fact that the fast is not a burden, not a punishment, but a gift of God's grace. . . . Our Lenten abstinence does not imply a rejection of God's creation . . . to fast is not to deny this intrinsic goodness but to reaffirm it."[11]

Whether applied in the area of entertainment, chastity, or scheduling, the words of Thomas Aquinas (1225–1274) hold true: "Abstinence pertains to the Kingdom of God only in so far as it proceeds from faith and the love of God."[12]

Today's Reading: John 19:17–27

_____

_____

_____

_____

_____

_____

_____

_____

_____

_____

DAY THIRTY-ONE

violent /ˈvaɪ(ə)lənt/ *adj.*

Of action, behaviour, etc.: characterized by the doing of deliberate harm or damage; carried out or accomplished using physical violence.[1]

mockery /ˈmɑk(ə)ri/ *n.*

Derision, ridicule; a mocking or derisive utterance or action.[2]

gnatius of Loyola (1491–1556) encouraged a method of Scripture meditation that included activating our imagination to create a "mental picture" of the scene we are reflecting upon and asking God to help us emotionally engage with the subject matter. He stated, "if [the meditation] is on the Passion, I ask for pain, tears, and suffering with Christ's suffering."[3] Centuries of worshipers have thickened their devotion by meditating upon Jesus' Passion Week suffering: the beatings, crowning with thorns, flogging, and crucifixion. Honestly, such meditations are difficult for me. My guess is that I am not alone in that confession. As far as thresholds for violence go, mine is very (very) low. As far as meditating upon what Jesus endured, well, I can barely type through my tears.

Get up and get going where?

Stop #6: Violent Mockery. The Gospel writers document four distinct groups that were emotionally and physically aggressive toward Jesus during His trials: Annas's official, the chief priests and Sanhedrin and their guards, Herod and his soldiers, and Pilate's soldiers. Today, I offer you a simple and sober compilation of the pre-crucifixion violent mockery Jesus suffered in His journey cross-ward. I invite you to consider each instance slowly with as much realism as you can bear.

> "The miracles did just what Jesus had predicted. To those who chose to believe him, they gave even more reason to believe. But for those determined to deny him, the miracles made little difference. Some things just have to be believed to be seen."
>
> —PHILIP YANCEY[4]

One of Annas's officials (John 18:22):

» "slapped him in the face."

The chief priests, Sanhedrin, and their guards:[5]

» "took him and beat him";
» "began mocking and beating him";
» "spit in his face";
» "blindfolded him";
» "slapped him";
» "struck him with their fists";
» "said, 'Prophesy to us, Christ. Who hit you?'";
» "said many other insulting things to him."

Herod and his soldiers (Luke 23:11):

» "ridiculed and mocked him";
» "[dressed] him in an elegant robe" and "sent him back to Pilate."

Pilate's soldiers:[6]

» "stripped him";
» "flogged" him;
» "put a scarlet robe on him";
» "twisted together a crown of thorns and set it on his head";
» "put a staff in his right hand and knelt in front of him and mocked him," saying, "Hail, king of the Jews!";
» "spit on him";
» "took the staff and struck him on the head again and again";
» "falling on their knees, they paid homage to him";
» "mocked him";
» "put his own clothes [back] on him."

Reflection

Is it not odd in a generation that rarely blinks at fictional violence sold as "entertainment" that we spend relatively little time considering the all-too-real suffering of our Savior? Picture once again what Jesus endured even prior to the crucifixion. Then go stand in front of mirror. Looking at yourself, say aloud these words: "Jesus endured His suffering for me. He believed—and still believes—that I am worth it."

Today's Fast: Mocking Jesus

Fast mocking Jesus? Who would ever do such a thing in the first place? Perhaps we would when we, like Annas's official, are more concerned with saving face than honoring truth. Perhaps we would when we, like the religious leaders, act as though Jesus is blindfolded and cannot see what we are doing. Perhaps we would when we, like the guards, use one of Jesus' names in vain. Perhaps we mock Jesus more than we know.

On Lent

Christian Initiation. When Jesus mercifully interrupted my existence, the church suddenly embraced me as one of their own. Though I was encouraged to "take the next step in water baptism," "become a member," and "attend Sunday school," there were no interviews to undergo, or classes to attend, or tests to pass. However, Patricia Mann,[7] citing Ambrose (AD 340–397) and Augustine (AD 354–430), refers to Christian Initiation[8] as a historically intense, five-stage process that culminated at Easter[9] in which the participants (*competentes*)

> Were expected to fast each day until the ninth hour. They also abstained from all meat and wine and kept their diet bland and simple. On Sundays and Holy Thursday, the fast was lifted, while on Holy Saturday, it was tightened so that they, together with all the faithful, would take neither food nor drink. . . . They also distributed alms and occasionally spent all night praying. Finally the *competentes* were not allowed to bathe—an ancient tradition alluded to as early as the *Apostolic Tradition.* This involved not only physical discomfort, but breaking with the social life of the public baths. The fast from bathing ended on Holy Thursday.[10]

Wow. (Yes, I know that sounds something less than academic, but, wow.) Ambrose and Augustine lived decades after The Great Persecution (AD 311–313) in which "to believe" meant "to the point of death." In the absence of the fires of persecution, rites of initiation may have helped ensure the sincerity of adherents in a world where favor is all too fragile.

Today's Reading: John 19:28–37

DAY THIRTY-TWO

He was despised and rejected by mankind,
a man of suffering, and familiar with pain.

—ISAIAH 53:3

A s affirmed in each Gospel, Pilate attempted to free Jesus multiple times. He repeatedly told the religious leaders that he found no basis for any charge against Jesus.[1] He gave the people the opportunity to choose Jesus as the one prisoner to release at the time of the Passover.[2] He tried to have Jesus punished and then freed.[3] And he appealed directly to the crowds, asking them what they wanted him to do with their king.[4] All Pilate's efforts failed, which brought Jesus to **Stop #7**: The Finalization of Rejection.

In addition to being rejected by the religious leaders, Jesus was rejected by the crowds twice. First, the crowds chose Barabbas over Jesus to receive the get-out-of-jail-free card, and in doing so, gave history the profoundly theological visual of Jesus dying in the place of sinners. Secondly, the crowds rejected Jesus en masse in an emotionally charged exchange with Pilate. Though in our day we are more than a little obsessed with exact times and sequences, ancient writers were often less linear in world-view and, consequently, actual events were sometimes listed in an order consistent with a theme as opposed to chronologically. Such is the case in the Gospels when Matthew and Mark placed this emotionally charged exchange before Jesus' flogging and John positioned this exchange after the flogging.[5]

Rome tortured its prisoners prior to execution, and it was not unusual for someone to die from a flogging before they ever made it to a cross.[6] Though Deuteronomy 25:3 limited flogging to forty lashes and the Talmudic Law reduced that limit by one to avoid accidental excess, Roman law possessed no such limitations.[7] Dr. Martin Hengel (1926–2009), professor of New Testament and early Judaism, stated in his classic work on crucifixion that, "the flogging that was a stereotyped part of the punishment would make the blood flow in streams."[8]

In John's account, after enduring however many lashes the Roman soldiers inflicted, Jesus was presented contemptuously adorned with a crown of thorns embedded in his head, a body brutalized by repeated blows, and a purple robe soaking up the trauma of His shredded back (John 19:5). As Pilate "sat down on the judge's seat at a place known as the Stone Pavement," (John 19:13) and said to the gathered mob, "Here is your king," Jesus stood facing the crowds as they replied with a roar, "Take him away! Take him away! Crucify him!" (John 19:15).

In 1876, Robert Lowry wrote a song called "Nothing but the Blood." The refrain reads:

> *Oh! precious is the flow*
> *That makes me white as snow;*
> *No other fount I know,*
> *Nothing but the blood of Jesus.*[9]

That precious flow began before, not on, the cross. Jesus' blood was shed at every point of rejection. Through fists and staffs and whips,

Jesus' blood fell in Caiaphas's house and Pilate's palace and every point in between. And when His rejection was complete, Pilate handed Jesus over to the soldiers for crucifixion, which fills in the map we began days ago with John 14:31. Get up and get going where? Cross-ward. The seed Jesus had spoken of in John 12:24 was falling to the ground to die. Though its destined fruitfulness was beyond the disciples' sight and even out of the reach of their faith, Jesus' followers were now only days away from a moment in which the Rejected would be revealed as the Redeemer.

> "'He humbled Himself'? Was He not on earth always stripping off first one robe of honor and then another, till, naked, He was fastened to the cross, and there did He not empty out His inmost self, pouring out His life-blood, giving up for all of us, till they laid Him penniless in a borrowed grave? How low was our dear Redeemer brought!"
>
> —C. H. SPURGEON (1834–1892)[10]

Reflection

As the faithful were preparing to celebrate the Passover, Jesus was preparing to offer Himself as the Lamb. Reflect on the following Scriptures with gratitude for the One John the Baptist called "The Lamb of God, who takes away the sin of the world!"[11]

> Tell the whole community of Israel that on the tenth day of this month each man is to take a lamb for his family, one for each household.... The animals you choose must be year-old males without defect.... Take care of them until the fourteenth day of the month, when all the people of the community of Israel must slaughter ... the Passover lamb. Take a bunch of hyssop, dip it into the blood in the basin and put some of the blood on the top and on both sides of the doorframe.... When the LORD goes through the land to strike down

the Egyptians, he will see the blood on the top and sides of the door-frame and will pass over that doorway, and he will not permit the destroyer to enter your houses and strike you down. (Exodus 12:3, 5–6, 21–23)

For you know that it was not with perishable things such as silver or gold that you were redeemed from the empty way of life handed down to you from your ancestors, but with the precious blood of Christ, a lamb without blemish or defect. (1 Peter 1:18–19)

Then I saw a Lamb, looking as if it had been slain, standing in the center of the throne, encircled by the four living creatures and the elders. . . . Each one had a harp and they were holding golden bowls full of incense, which are the prayers of God's people. And they sang a new song, saying:

"You are worthy to take the scroll
and to open its seals,
because you were slain,
and with your blood you purchased for God
persons from every tribe and language and people and
nation." (Revelation 5:6, 8–9)

Today's Fast: Addition

Jesus is enough. His shed blood was sufficient for our salvation. Adding to Him only distracts us. In the prologue, I spoke of sins of addition: "adding niceties and luxuries to our list of basic needs, adding imaginations onto the strong back of vision, adding self-satisfaction to the purity of peace." Jesus' yoke is easy and His burden is light (Matthew 11:29–30). Our additions are not.

In honor of Jesus' loss of blood for your soul, and toward sensitizing yourself to ways in which you are adding what is unnecessary to your faith, fast adding anything to life today. Try to spend a day without spending money. Let each choice to not buy remind you of what you could not purchase: your pardon.

On Lent

Visual thinning. Lent is a thinning season. The tradition calls us to less, not more; to decrease, not increase; to simplify, not amplify. A beautiful image of this thinning occurs in the Orthodox church on Cheese-fare Sunday as the cry ". . . for I am afflicted!" fills the church, and then, as Schmemann describes so beautifully, "Lent is here! Bright vestments are put aside; lights are extinguished. . . . We will have to wander forty days through the desert of Lent."[12] In the Catholic tradition, the altar is ungraced by flowers during Lent and even the music simplifies[13] as silence is welcomed. Robin Jensen adds that:

> Prior to the revision of the liturgy mandated by Vatican II, Roman Catholic churches typically veiled their crosses and statuary for the last two weeks, only uncovering them during the singing of the Gloria in the Easter Vigil. Other practices in the more liturgical churches, such as "bidding farewell to the Alleluia," banning floral arrangements, avoiding instrumental music, and limiting festivity at weddings expressed the penitential nature of the season in many Christian traditions.[14]

Like the restrained and unaccompanied music of Lent, the simplifying of our visual environment helps us to settle into a contemplative mood and encourages us to focus. Our thoughts turn inward; our actions are measured, our diet spare.[15]

Today's Reading: John 19:38–42

_____

_____

_____

_____

_____

_____

_____

_____

_____

_____

_____

_____

_____

DAY THIRTY-THREE

"his hour" was still not over. "This cup" was still full of suffering. With the blood of the new covenant trailing behind Him, Jesus walked from the Praetorium in Jerusalem to Golgotha. Countless pilgrims have sought to retrace Jesus' agonizing steps alone with the Scriptures, in respectful silence before Stations of the Cross,[1] and even along the Via Dolorosa in Jerusalem. Why linger in the pain so many centuries after Christ's resurrection? Because it was real. Perhaps we would live differently if we remembered more frequently (and more accurately) what the cross cost.

After Pilate handed Jesus over to his soldiers for crucifixion, his soldiers led Jesus out of the city. Historically, "a soldier at the head of the procession carried the *titulus*, an inscription written on wood, which stated the defendant's name and the crime for which he had been condemned" and was affixed to the cross during crucifixion.[2] By Pilate's command, and with disregard of religious leaders' protests, Jesus' *titulus* read, "Jesus of Nazareth: The king of the Jews."[3] Once the company arrived outside the city at the place where Rome executed its prisoners, all four Gospels starkly state, "they crucified him."[4]

Crucifixion was not a Roman invention. Eastern cultures—such as Assyria, Phoenicia, and Persia—employed crucifixion for almost a thousand years before Rome officially adopted the method for use with non-Roman criminals.[5] Rome utilized the punishment liberally, at first among slaves, and then later

> . . . To punish foreign captives, rebels and fugitives, especially during times of war and rebellion. Captured enemies and rebels were crucified in masses. . . . After the Romans quelled the relatively minor rebellion in Judea in 7 A. D. triggered by the death of King Herod, Quintilius Varus, the Roman Legate of Syria, crucified 2,000 Jews in Jerusalem. During Titus's siege of Jerusalem in 70 A. D., Roman troops crucified as many as 500 Jews a day for several months.[6]

Though Pilate used water to symbolically wash responsibility off his hands (Matthew 27:24), his soldiers used water to wash very real blood off their hands daily. Crucifixion was part of the job. What we call Good Friday was simply another day of work to them. Hengel explained that though most Roman crucifixions included "a flogging beforehand, and the victim often carried his own beam to the place of execution, where he was nailed to it with outstretched arms, and raised up and seated on a small wooden peg," methodology still varied somewhat because the "caprice and sadism of the executioners [was] given full rein."[7]

> "'It's God who ought to suffer, not you and me,' say those who bear a grudge against God for the unfairness of life. The curse word expresses it well: God be damned. And on that day, God was damned. The cross that held Jesus' body, naked and marked with scars, exposed all the violence and injustice of this world. At once, the Cross revealed what kind of world we have and what kind of God we have: a world of gross unfairness, a God of sacrificial love."
>
> —PHILIP YANCEY[8]

Allow me to quote at length from Greek archeologist, Dr. Vassilios Tzaferis (d. 2015)[9] who studied the remains of a Jewish man crucified by the Romans[10] sometime before AD 70:

> Without any supplementary body support, the victim would die from muscular spasms and asphyxia in a very short time, certainly within two or three hours.... In order to prolong the agony, Roman executioners devised two instruments that would keep the victim alive on the cross for extended periods of time. One, known as a *sedile*, was a small seat attached to the front of the cross, about halfway down. This device provided some support for the victim's body.... Both Erenaeus and Justin Martyr describe the cross of Jesus as having five extremities rather than four; the fifth was probably the *sedile*. To increase the victim's suffering, the *sedile* was pointed, thus inflicting horrible pain.[11]

Jesus' breath had jump-started Adam's life but now Jesus, paying for the sins of Adam and his descendants, was struggling for air. With bones nailed to the cross and blood pouring from His wounds, the "author of life" (Acts 3:15), through Whom "all things were created" (Colossians 1:16), was dying.

Our jewelry-studded crosses did not prepare us for this. Perhaps more than other ages, we must work to see Jesus in Golgotha. Church history beckons us to soberly consider Jesus' sacrifice and be humbled anew by the prophetic words of Isaiah spoken some seven centuries before Golgotha:

> Surely he took up our pain
> and bore our suffering,
> yet we considered him punished by God,
> stricken by him, and afflicted.
> But he was pierced for our transgressions,

he was crushed for our iniquities;
the punishment that brought us peace was upon him,
and by his wounds we are healed. (Isaiah 53:4–5)

Reflection

Today, along with the words of Isaiah 53 above, consider the words King David penned over a thousand years before Jesus' crucifixion in preparation for tomorrow's reading. I encourage you to read all of Psalm 22, some of which I have excerpted below:

My God, my God, why have you forsaken me?
Why are you so far from saving me, from the words of my groaning? . . .
But I am a worm, and not a man,
scorned by everyone, despised by the people.
All who see me mock me;
they hurl insults, shaking their heads;
"He trusts in the LORD," they say, "let the LORD rescue him.
Let him deliver him, since he delights in him." . . .
I am poured out like water,
and all my bones are out of joint;
My heart has turned to wax;
it has melted within me; . . .
They pierce my hands and feet—
All my bones are on display—
People stare and gloat over me.
They divide my clothes among them,
 and cast lots for my garment. (Psalm 22: 1, 6–8, 14, 16–18)

Today's Fast: Willful Sin

Jesus died for our sin. Why then do we work to keep it alive? What benefit do we perceive ourselves receiving? Does that benefit outweigh the cost Christ paid? This is not a simplistic call to stop sinning. No, this is a sincere call for us to start loving Jesus to a degree that compels us to walk away from sin where we can and get help where we cannot. Today, in the shadow of Christ's crucifixion, offer this prayer to Jesus:

> Savior, am I caressing anything you were crucified for?
> If so, I repent: forgive me, heal me, send help
> to me, and strengthen my love for You.
> When I am tempted, may I see Your cross, remember Your cost,
> and let love "bind my wandering heart" to You.[12]

On Lent

Lenten words, part one. We now turn our attention to a collection of Lenten images and descriptions, organized chronologically, which together paint a picture of the many-layered meanings of the Lenten tradition. Since many ancient quotes have already been considered, the collection that follows contains only a few early quotes and an emphasis on modern interpretations. As you read, consider the progress of Lenten meaning in the church.

> Lent has oftentimes been likened by the Church Fathers as a spiritual journey of the soul with her Bridegroom through the wilderness of the world to her final resting place in the heavens.[13]
> Yet now is the time when the souls of all men should be urged

with greater earnestness towards spiritual progress, and animated with fuller confidence: now when the return of that day on which we were redeemed invites us to every work of piety, so that purified in body and soul we may celebrate that mystery which excels all others, the passion of our Lord.[14] (5th Century)

Today's Reading: John 20:1–9

_____

_____

_____

_____

_____

_____

_____

_____

_____

_____

DAY THIRTY-FOUR

Pilate's soldiers affixed Jesus to the cross at "the third hour," which meant three hours after sunrise, that is, perhaps around 9 a.m.[1] (Mark 15:25, NASB). Wood and nails fastened His bones firmly against the cross as gravity and loss of blood brought His life to an end. Jesus had six hours to live. Who would you surround yourself with if you had six hours to live? Our decorative nativity scenes depict the characters who surrounded Jesus at His birth: Joseph and Mary, a star, angels (who, more accurately, appeared in the nearby field), shepherds, Magi (who actually arrived much later), and a handful of remarkably well-behaved animals (which are not mentioned in the Scriptures at all but are simply too endearing to leave out). There is no blood—though after a birth there should have been. There are no nails—though within the manger that held Jesus there could have been.

Timothy Murphy captures some of this tension in his poem, *Address to the Manger*:

> Sleep, infant, sleep
> among the oxen and the sheep
> which kneel before your manger.
> Welcome to danger.

When you become a man
preach us the Good News while you can
before you bear the scourge and cross,
an everlasting loss

we all bear to the grave
with guilt. It was your doom to save
us sinners, us ungodly men
whose sins slay you again.

You could have claimed your own
Egypt, a Pharaoh's golden throne.
Instead, child, you are humbly born
as Gabriel blows his horn.[2]

Yes, Jesus, "welcome to [the] danger." In the absence of a nativity-like heirloom to help us visualize the scene of Jesus' death, we shall construct our own.

Seven distinct groups surrounded Jesus at His crucifixion at varying distances. On the outermost edge was a group of *passersby* who "hurled insults at him, shaking their heads and saying, 'You who are going to destroy the temple and build it in three days, save yourself! Come down from the cross, if you are the Son of God!'"[3] Neither interested enough to stay nor compassionate enough to be quiet, this group tossed taunts from afar and then continued on their way.

Also at a safe distance, but silenced by grief, was a group of *unnamed disciples*, described as "those who knew him, including the women who had followed him from Galilee," who "stood at a distance, watching these things" (Luke 23:49). Jesus' life had transformed them. They would not leave Him until by death He left first.

Closer in were two groups that may have stood as one: *watchers* and *rulers.* Watchers, well, watched, and on occasion offered commentaries like "He's calling Elijah,"[4] or "Now leave him alone. Let's see if Elijah comes to save him."[5] Though one of the watchers became a wild-haired activist at one point and ran to offer Jesus a sponge of wine vinegar on a stick,[6] this group spoke about Jesus but not to Jesus. The *rulers*—which included chief priests, teachers of the law, and the elders—echoed the taunts of the passersby with a few more digs: "Let him come down now from the cross, and we will believe in him. He trusts in God. Let God rescue him now if he wants him, for he said, 'I am the Son of God.'"[7]

"If God wants him": my soul responds to the phrase with fire. In the face of such a taunt, it becomes clear that love, not nails, kept Jesus on the cross: love and how much *He* wanted *us.* Some in the three closer groups understood, or were about to understand, that truth far more clearly.

> "Lord, make me a channel of your peace. Where there is hatred let me bring your love; where there is injury your pardon; where there is doubt, true faith in you. Where there is despair in life, let me bring hope; where there is darkness only light; where there is sadness, ever joy. Grant that I may never cease so much to be consoled as to console; to be understood as to understand, to be loved, as to love with all my soul. It is in pardoning that we are pardoned, in giving to all men what we receive, and in dying that we are born to eternal life."
>
> —POPULARLY ATTRIBUTED TO SAINT FRANCIS OF ASSISI (1182–1226)[9]

Reflection

These were not original taunts. Jesus had heard them before in the wilderness temptation.[8] Today, place yourself at the foot of the cross and, from that perspective, hear the taunts of those who hurled insults at Him. Then reflect on the reality that Jesus' name is still mocked and despised today.

Today's Fast: Criticism

Though occasionally accomplished constructively through calmly asser-tive conversation, criticism is often a cowardly act. Criticism knows a little, assumes a lot, and airs judgments with conviction as did the *rulers* and the *passersby*: "It's your own fault that you are there. You have no one to blame but yourself. You said this. You did that. You deserve what you got."

How often have we passed by Jesus, or watched Him from a safe dis-tance, and hurled such insults? We hope never . . . and then read Jesus' words:

> I was hungry and you gave me nothing to eat, I was thirsty and you
> gave me nothing to drink, I was a stranger and you did not invite
> me in, I needed clothes and you did not clothe me, I was sick and in
> prison and you did not look after me. . . . Truly I tell you, whatever
> you did not do for one of the least of these, you did not do for me.
> (Matthew 25:42–43, 45)

"It's their own fault . . . they got what they deserved," we say as we pass by "the least of these."

Today, fast criticism. From the clerk moving slowly to the homeless vet on the streets, consider carefully that Jesus knows them by name. Today, seek to know more, assume less, and air prayers for Jesus' "least of these" boldly in the presence of your shared Father God.

On Lent

Lenten words, part two. Today we continue our consideration of Lenten quotes.

God does not ask or desire that a person should mourn from sorrow of heart, but rather that out of love for Him he should rejoice with spiritual joy. . . . As I ponder the true nature of compunction, I find myself amazed by the way in which inward joy and gladness mingle with what we call mourning and grief, like honey in a comb. There must be a lesson here and it surely is that compunction is properly a gift from God, so that there is real pleasure in the soul, since God secretly brings consolation to those who in their hearts are repenting.[10] (6th Century)

But mortification—literally, "making death"—is what life is all about, a slow discovery of the mortality of all that is created so that we can appreciate its beauty without clinging to it as if it were a lasting possession. . . . In every arrival there is a leave-taking; in every reunion there is a separation; in each one's growing up there is a growing old; in every smile there is a tear; and in every success there is a loss. All living is dying, and all celebration is mortification too.[11] (1992)

Lent is a time for introspection and spiritual candor. Believers are to acknowledge our complicity in the deep brokenness of the world, seek to amend our lives, and wait in hope for the healing grace of our God.[12] (2012)

Today's Reading: John 20:10–18

_____

_____

_____

_____

_____

DAY THIRTY-FIVE

Close enough to Jesus to hear His voice as He struggled for air was yet another group. These *named disciples* included "his mother, his mother's sister, Mary the wife of Clopas, and Mary Magdalene ... and the disciple whom He loved" (John 19:25–26). From John's account, Jesus' impending death seems to have left Mary in need of a protector, and so Jesus entrusted His mother to His dearest friend.

Another group near Jesus witnessed His death because they had no choice: "*Two rebels* were crucified with him, one on his right and one on his left."[1] From the cross, Jesus only directly addressed people twice: first as just noted above, and then again, to one of the rebels. Whereas Matthew and Mark's gospels stated that, "those crucified with him also heaped insults on him,"[2] Luke recorded insults from one man and an inquiry from the other. We have no means of knowing how much of Jesus' story this second rebel knew, but it was evident to him that Jesus had "done nothing wrong." From one dying man to another he asked, "Remember me when you come into your kingdom" (Luke 23:41–42). Surely this is among the most insightful statements of faith in Christ in the Gospels, for this dying man discerned that Jesus' kingdom was not of this world.

The closest group to Jesus physically, however, was probably the *soldiers* who guarded him. Like the *passersby* and the *rulers*, they mocked Him (Luke 23:36–37). Like the *watchers*, they spoke about Jesus, but not to Jesus, as they cast lots for His garment (John 19:23–24). Jesus was, after all, their job, not their God. They were close to Jesus because they were paid to be close to Jesus. This last and nearest group was, therefore, present in body, but not in spirit, until the earth began to shake: "It was now about the sixth hour, and darkness fell over the whole land until the ninth hour, for the sun was obscured."[3] Then Jesus cried out in a loud voice and died.[4] At that moment, "the curtain of the temple was torn in two from top to bottom,"[5] "the earth shook, the rocks split," and "the tombs broke open. The bodies of many holy people who had died were raised to life" (Matthew 27:51–52). Imagine!

> "I know of three classes of people among those who are being saved: slaves, employees, and sons. If you are a slave, fear punishment; if you are an employee, look only for wages; if you are more than these—if you are a son—then revere God as Father. Do what is good because it is good to obey a Father. And even if there will be no reward for you, it is reward enough to have pleased your Father. Let us then take care not to despise these things."
>
> —GREGORY OF NAZIANZUS (379–381)[6]

And how did each of the seven groups surrounding Jesus respond? The Scriptures only answer that question in part. The *passersby* had perhaps already passed. The *unnamed disciples* remained mournfully at their distant post.[7] The *watchers* "beat their breasts and went away" (Luke 23:48). The *rulers* likewise appear to have left, assuming, understandably, that Jesus' death ended His life.[8] The *named disciples* may have collapsed with grief while the *rebels* continued their struggle to breathe.[9] And the *soldiers*? "When the centurion and those with him who were guarding Jesus saw the earthquake and all that had happened, they were terrified, and exclaimed, 'Surely he was the Son of God!'" (Matthew 27:54).[10]

Yes, the earth shook, but why did the centurion and his men associate it with Jesus' death? What else had they seen? What else had they heard? What moved them to such a proclamation of faith? They witnessed Jesus' death, not His life. They had heard His moanings, not seen His miracles. Yet even Jesus' dying moments defined Him well. What the rulers saw as defeat, Jesus saw as the finish line. With His "It is finished,"[11] Jesus entered triumphantly into death.

Reflection

Together, the seven groups create quite a collage of humanity: men and women, Jew and Gentile, rulers and death-row outcasts, mothers and soldiers, doubters and disciples, the spiritually poor rich and the spiritually rich poor, and scoffers and seekers. Imagine Jesus seeing each group, bleeding for each group, and dying for each group. Imagine Christ on the cross with open pierced arms for us all.

Today's Fast: God-as-job

Paid to be close to Jesus: nearest and yet farthest away. The paycheck can change your perspective whether paid in cash or in praise. The soldiers valued Jesus' stuff more than His life. As they kept themselves busy around the cross, they numbed themselves to His voice.

Today, fast God-as-job. Whether your check comes from a church or not, consider ways in which you, too, may be near in body but absent in spirit, taking care of Jesus' stuff but not attending to His voice. Proximity does not automate intimacy. Only love transforms "near" into "for."

On Lent

Lenten words, part three. Today we will continue our reflection upon Lenten quotes.

> The Lenten season offers us once again an opportunity to reflect upon the very heart of Christian life: charity. This is a favorable time to renew our journey of faith, both as individuals and as a community, with the help of the word of God and the sacraments. This journey is one marked by prayer and sharing, silence and fasting, in anticipation of the joy of Easter.[12] (2012)

> When most of us think of Lent, we immediately think about giving something up—sugar, TV, radio, you name it. . . . Lent is packed with special services and religious practices to help us focus on the life of Christ—more prayer, more devotional reading, more church services. . . . Amid all the devotion, however, the last thing we think of adding to our Lenten disciplines is observing the Sabbath. This is surprising, since the Bible seems to teach that rest may be the most significant and transformative activity of all.[13] (2012)

> What does Lent mean to me personally? It's a time of soul-searching. Am I doing the best that I can to live up to the teachings of Christ? If not, then I do need the penance, I do need the fasting, I do need to remind myself that I am supposed to be following in the footsteps of Christ. Not just because I'm a priest but because I'm a Catholic Christian. And it's meant to also be a time of identifying more closely with the poor.[14] (2013)

Today's Reading: John 20:19–23

_____

_____

_____

_____

_____

_____

_____

_____

_____

_____

_____

_____

_____

DAY THIRTY-SIX

O ne Joseph held Jesus at His birth. Another Joseph held Jesus at His death."[1] All four Gospels recorded Joseph of Arimathea's service to Jesus.[2] From these accounts we learn that Joseph was a member of the Jewish Council publicly and a disciple of Jesus privately. A man of integrity who sought God's will and ways, Joseph had not endorsed the Council's decision to condemn Jesus. Up until the crucifixion, Joseph had kept his commitment to Jesus a secret for fear of those with whom he ruled. But as Jesus breathed His last, Joseph went boldly to Pilate and requested Jesus' body. Summoning the same centurion who had exclaimed at Jesus' death, "Surely this man was the Son of God!" (Mark 15:39), Pilate asked for a confirmation that Jesus had passed, and "when he learned from the centurion that it was so, he gave the body to Joseph" (Mark 15:45). Accompanied by Nicodemus, Joseph then returned to Golgotha, removed Jesus' body from the cross, and prepared it respectfully for a burial.

Citing the author of Ecclesiastes' conviction that it is better to be "a stillborn child" than a man who "does not receive proper burial" (Ecclesiastes 6:3), Dr. Mark Davis discussed Joseph of Arimathea's actions from the perspective of this ancient association between "burial and blessedness":

When read in light of the burial practices of the Hebrew Bible, Joseph is making a significant statement by requesting the body of Jesus, preparing it for burial, and then burying it in a newly hewn tomb. Bearing in mind that Jesus had just been put to death because he was accused of being both an enemy of God and an enemy of the state, Joseph's actions would seem awfully close to treason or blasphemy, because they protest that Jesus' life was in fact honorable.... Understood through the prism of the Hebrew Bible, Matthew 27:57–66 is more than an account of a touching gesture after the nightmare of the crucifixion. It is the story of a bold declaration, by a religious leader who has much to lose, that the life of the condemned and crucified Jesus was honorable.[3]

Joseph risked his reputation and possibly his freedom to honor a dead man. With the help of Nicodemus, he wrapped Jesus' body with new linens and seventy-five pounds of spices. Then he placed the body in a tomb—but not just any tomb. Joseph placed Jesus in his own tomb, a "new tomb that he had cut out of the rock" (Matthew 27:60). Joseph of Arimathea gave Jesus his resting place. It was a treasured, costly space reserved for himself, but Joseph gifted it to Jesus. Further, Joseph gave this risk-laden treasure to Jesus at a time when Jesus could not—from Joseph's perspective—do anything else for him.

> As I see the body, I believe its parts,
> as I prepare its presence and final place
> praying against the rigidity, as I
> confirm each cut and document his death.
> I anoint with balm and Jewish rite.
> How can these things be, our need
> displayed among his torso, head, and palms?
> I'm healing when it's too late to forgive,
> cowering in psalms I've tried to live,
> as the cold harrows the skin, the linen
> bloodless and dry and beautifully stitched.
> In midnight's pattern I've come to believe
> in how to keep his image fresh and here
> while we suffer. While he needs to sleep.
>
> —NEIL AZEVEDO[4]

Joseph's actions stir something within me: an ache possibly too deep for words. I long for Jesus to occupy my resting place. Whatever part *of me* I have reserved *for me*—for my self—I long to give it away to Jesus. When we offer to Jesus the place we have reserved for our *selves*, He surprises us by filling that space with His resurrected life. By offering his resting place to Jesus, Joseph transformed a tomb from a place of death for himself into a place of victory for His God.

Reflection

Focus today upon Joseph's change of heart. What do you guess happened within Joseph's mind and spirit that inspired him to boldly and publicly honor Jesus at His death?

Today's Fast: Withholding

As seen in the example of Joseph of Arimathea, offering our very *selves* to Jesus may seem foolish to others and quite costly to us. But there comes a point in relationship with God where in order for love to keep growing, another restrictive layer of self-protection must be discarded. In that moment, maintaining patterns of withholding will snuff out devotion and a choice simply must be made. Joseph chose to risk it all for love.

Today, fast withholding. Ask God to reveal any area in which you are withholding love from Him, others, or yourself. Though discerning the "whys" of our withholding patterns is immensely helpful, change is not at the mercy of our understanding. So, take a step, take a risk, and offer Jesus, to an even deeper degree, all that you have reserved for your *self*.

On Lent

Lenten words, part four. From Pope Leo the Great's (d. 461) focus on the Lord's passion to Pope Benedict XVI's (1927—) focus on charity; from the sixth-century embrace of godly grief to the twenty-first-century emphasis on personal soul-searching; from the early church fathers' journey through the wilderness to more recent invitations to rest; even from late-twentieth-century Nouwen's call to godly mortification to an early twenty-first-century Yale divinity professor's call for introspection and healing, the ancient image of a Lenten season focused upon a communal, purifying, sacrificial fellowship with the Lord's suffering seems to have given way to something more individualized and less strenuous.

Fr. Taft eloquently summarizes the challenge of Lenten understanding in the current age:

> Of course it is hard to die to self when we don't know who we are—a very special modern problem—but this should not deter us, for in opening ourselves to the Christ in others we discover who we are in the deepest sense of the word, far more deeply than by the superficial path of self-affirmation that comes from the insecurity of an undetermined self-image.[5]

> The problem is a broad and complicated one. There is, first, the very problematic of penance and asceticism for modern men and women—a problem which, unlike the Protestant rejection of penance, comes from modern psychology, and the quest for meaning and sincerity in an increasingly dehumanized technological world. Modern Christians reject penance and asceticism because they often lead to the distortion or destruction of more important human values. Hard things are not necessarily good things. . . . And anyway, what is the value of self-inflicted pain for modern men and women whose whole drive is to eliminate pain, to develop in freedom the autonomous self?[6]

Perhaps in our day, a rediscovery of Lent may help marry the modern celebration of grace with the mystery of sacrificial love treasured by the ancients.

Today's Reading: John 20:24–31

_____

_____

_____

_____

_____

_____

_____

_____

_____

_____

While Mary Magdalene and Mary the mother of Joseph[1] watched, Joseph and Nicodemus closed the tomb with a large stone. They did not have much time to linger. The Gospels state in unison that it was Preparation Day and the Sabbath was about to begin.[2] The writers obviously understood what this meant. Centuries later, however, we are sadly less familiar with Sabbaths in general and Preparation Days in particular. The distance is more than definitional. Interpreting scriptural time references from the perspective of a culture organized around a Gregorian, instead of Jewish, calendar can be challenging.

The Jewish year (based upon the cycle of the moon) is 354 days, whereas the Gregorian year (based upon the cycle of the sun) is 365. Neither exactly matches their respective cycles, which is why an extra month (Adar II) is added every two to

> "If the enemy forces us to give up our quietness, we must not listen to him. For nothing is like quietness and abstinence from food. They combine to fight together against him. For they give keen insight to the inner eyes."
>
> —ABBA DOULAS
> (C. 3RD CENTURY)[3]

three years to the former and an extra day (February 29) is added every four years to the latter. Jesus' culture—as directed in Leviticus 23:32—counted a "day" from sunset to sunset, whereas we start (but do not begin) a new day at midnight. Within each day, the actual "hour" varied depending upon when the sun rose,[4] whereas we fix our hours independently of cycles of light and dark. Additionally, some scholars move the crucifixion up a day by proposing that Passion Week had two Sabbaths due to the Passover (which is called the *Great Shabbat*) landing that year in proximity to the regular weekly Shabbat.[5]

Nonetheless, today most communities of faith remember Jesus' death on Good Friday and spend the next days contemplating what it meant for Christ to be crucified, which is how I suppose the days were spent by Joseph, Nicodemus, Mary, and the rest of the disciples. Today I invite you to reflect upon two poems. The second is a modern, very personal response to the day of Jesus' death. The first is an ancient, highly prophetic description of God's Suffering Servant. As you read, consider the how and why of Jesus' holy decrease.

ISAIAH 53

Who has believed our message
    and to whom has the arm of the LORD been revealed?
He grew up before him like a tender shoot,
    and like a root out of dry ground.
He had no beauty or majesty to attract us to him,
    nothing in his appearance that we should desire him.
He was despised and rejected by mankind,
    a man of suffering, and familiar with pain.
Like one from whom people hide their faces
    he was despised, and we held him in low esteem.
Surely he took up our pain
    and bore our suffering,

yet we considered him punished by God,
 stricken by him, and afflicted.
But he was pierced for our transgressions,
 he was crushed for our iniquities;
the punishment that brought us peace was on him,
 and by his wounds we are healed.
We all, like sheep, have gone astray,
 each of us has turned to our own way;
and the LORD has laid on him
 the iniquity of us all.
He was oppressed and afflicted,
 yet he did not open his mouth;
he was led like a lamb to the slaughter,
 and as a sheep before its shearers is silent,
 so he did not open his mouth.
By oppression and judgment he was taken away.
 Yet who of his generation protested?
For he was cut off from the land of the living;
 for the transgression of my people he was punished.
He was assigned a grave with the wicked,
 and with the rich in his death,
though he had done no violence,
 nor was any deceit in his mouth.
Yet it was the LORD's will to crush him and cause him to suffer,
 and though the LORD makes his life an offering for sin,
he will see his offspring and prolong his days,
 and the will of the LORD will prosper in his hand.
After he has suffered,
 he will see the light of life and be satisfied;
by his knowledge my righteous servant will justify many,
 and he will bear their iniquities.
Therefore I will give him a portion among the great,

and he will divide the spoils with the strong,
because he poured out his life unto death,
and was numbered with the transgressors.
For he bore the sin of many,
and made intercession for the transgressors.

PREPARATION DAY

the dove which nests in the cleft
of a wound in which I've a part
is a whiteness gently resting
before a quiet, broken heart
below the cross is room to love
the time of dying a loss endured
behind a stone his body laid
the mercy of God thus immured
sorrow wrapped around his bones
his skin shines whiter than the shroud
in the newness of a borrowed tomb
the promise of love is a space allowed
the suffering of the wound of love
is a loneliness which I have made
within my weeping, contrite heart
there his pierced heart is laid

—SEAN KINSELLA[6]

Reflection

The high priest carries the blood of animals into the Most Holy Place as a sin offering, but the bodies are burned outside the camp. And so Jesus also suffered outside the city gate to make the people holy through his own blood. Let us, then, go to him outside the camp, bearing the disgrace he bore.

—HEBREWS 13:11–13

Today, go "outside the camp" with Jesus. Meditate upon the appalling way in which He died. Ponder the grace His death purchased. Mourn over those who still reject Him today.

Today's Fast: Your Voice

When tragedy strikes, communities honor the fallen with a moment of silence. Today we will honor Jesus' sacrifice in the same way. Select a time period that is doable—be that an hour, an afternoon, or even a day—to fast your voice (talking, typing, and texting). As you begin your fast, hear Jesus say, "It is finished" and see Him "bow His head" and "give up His spirit" (John 19:30). Then honor Jesus with a period of focused quietness.

How? Have you ever been silenced by a painting, symphony, or play? Have you ever been moved so deeply by an experience that words failed you and the only worthy offering was silence? In fasting our voice we are focusing—not remotely emptying—our minds to behold Jesus with love. Be forewarned though: silence can be rather loud (as anyone who has attempted a silent retreat can affirm). As Brother Lawrence encouraged,

> If your mind wanders or withdraws from the Lord, do not be upset or disquieted. Trouble and disquiet serve more to distract the mind further from God than to recollect it. The will must bring the mind back in tranquility.[7]

Join the disciples today in beholding Jesus in His death. Our silence today will soon enough give way to celebration.

On Lent

In Conclusion, part one: In 1983 (the year this former atheist came to Christ), Fr. Taft compared Tertullian spirituality to the mood of his age, concluding:

> [Tertullian spirituality] is radically different from the incarnational spirituality prevalent for the past thirty years, which tells us that since God became man Christ is in our neighbor, and the real work of Christian spirituality is not to leave the world but to dive in and grab life with both hands. Justice is more important than mortification, love more important than celibacy, and so on. One result of this contemporary spiritual ideology is that it has dealt a death blow to fasting, penance, mortification. Today among contemporary religious one hears more of gourmet cooking than of fasting—a striking counter-symbol to anyone even superficially acquainted with the spiritual literature at the origins of religious life. And yet the season of Lent is still a major part of the liturgical year. Can such a season of penance have any real meaning for us today?[8]

Tertullian (c. 150–c. 212) is often quoted in relation to his conviction that God's Word was the only safe source of truth on earth. God-followers are citizens not of earth but of "the city above . . . [who] have nothing to do with the joys of the world; nay, [who] are called to the very opposite. . . . And I think the Lord affirms, that those who mourn are happy, not those who are crowned."[9] Roger E. Olson juxtaposes Tertullian with Clement of Alexandria, who though he honored the supremacy of the Scriptures, believed that "all truth is God's truth wherever it may be found."[10]

Today's Reading: John 21:1–9

_____

_____

_____

_____

_____

_____

_____

_____

_____

_____

_____

_____

_____

DAY THIRTY-EIGHT

The eternal weight of the space between Jesus' death and resurrection will only be known on the other side of this life, for the scriptural references are filled with both majesty and mystery.[1] Though Jesus' full assignment in those days is beyond our comprehension, the disciples' disillusionment is not. As we consider their journey, let us be attentive to our own, for we, too, understand what it means to bury dreams.[2] We, too, have thought our dreams were God's dreams and, consequently, prayed, believed, made plans, and worked hard. And then suddenly, it was over, and we sat graveside, by lifeless hopes, as the doubting began: "Did I miss something? Should I have prayed or done more? If *this* was not God's will, then I know nothing about hearing the voice of God."

The first followers understood. They, too, had a dream that was cruelly crucified before their very eyes. They were certain that their dream was God's dream but then their hoped-for Messiah was murdered. Not even a fool could hope now. The sealed tomb confirmed the truth: Jesus was dead. Today we speed-read through the darkest days of the disciples' lives because the joy of the resurrection is only a few verses away. But if we slow down there is much to learn. What did they do after their dream died on the cross? How did they cope? Let us walk with the disciples as they mourned the death of the greatest dream they had ever known.

Speechless, Jesus' followers kept watch until the very end (Luke 23:49). They held on to flickering hope until its flame was extinguished. Then they gave themselves permission to bury their dream. Burial is a symbol of respect. When dreams shatter, we, too, need to give ourselves time to gently collect the broken pieces and wrap them respectfully in tears. This is not about prematurely abandoning hope. This is about accepting reality. Denying Jesus' death would not return Him to the disciples. It was healthy for them to permit a burial. Faith is not threatened by funerals.

> The women . . . followed Joseph and saw the tomb and how his body was laid in it. Then they went home and prepared spices and perfumes. But they rested on the Sabbath in obedience to the command. (Luke 23:55–56)

Jesus' followers observed His tomb and returned home to prepare spices that would preserve and honor Jesus in His death. Then they rested. Rest is essential—a need, not a luxury—if we are to remain healthy through the burial of dreams. In the words of Rabbi Abraham Joshua Heschel (1907–1972), "Labor is a craft, but perfect rest is an art."[3] Those who have lost loved ones may need to linger in that favorite old chair. The one who suffered a miscarriage may need to give herself permission to mourn instead of rushing to put everything away. The entrepreneur may need unhurried days (instead of one angry hour) to reminisce as he packs up an office after an unsuccessful business venture. Take the time. Prepare the spices. Preserve and honor the memories. And rest.

"Now that same day two of them were going to a village called Emmaus. . . . They were talking with each other about everything that had happened" (Luke 24:13–14). The disciples did not isolate themselves after Jesus' burial, but intentionally maintained their relationships. We, too, must resist isolation and enjoy good talks and take long walks with trusted friends. For even in loss, we are stronger together than alone. Like the early disciples, as we walk and talk with each other, Jesus walks and talks with us (Luke 24:15–16). Walking with the Savior, they eventually realized that their dream, though dead, had not perished!

Most of us will not see the resurrection of our dreams within three days. In fact, some of our dreams are sown for future generations to reap. Even then, obedience is never a waste; it is an investment in a future we cannot see. When we dream with God, our dreams—even in burial— are not lost: they are planted. God never forgets the "kernel of wheat [that] falls to the ground and dies" (John 12:24).

> "Could it be that a legitimate stage of hope is hopelessness?"
>
> —DR. A. J. SWOBODA[4]

What grows from that painful planting is God's business. But sowing in faith is ours and, like the early disciples, our faithfulness is never sown in vain.

Reflection

Have you buried any dreams lately? If so, personalize each of the steps above and make space today to remember or rest or talk with friends. As you do, picture Jesus walking with the early disciples then and with you today. Many testify that His comfort intensifies graveside.

Today's Fast: Escapism

What is your default when spiritually disappointed? Some seek to distract themselves with activity. A few drown themselves with pity. Many numb themselves with entertainment. All are forms of escapism. For the health of our souls, we must resist checking out when it looks like God just died. He is still present and we must work to remain present too.

Today, fast escapism. Instead of distracting yourself with activity, cancel appointments to make space to be still. Instead of drowning yourself with pity, address God directly and honestly about your ache. Instead of numbing yourself with entertainment, let the pain be a reminder that you still need time to heal. Today, embrace the discomfort of disappointment as a noble step in your spiritual formation.

On Lent

In Conclusion, part two: Reflecting on Fr. Taft's concerns for my generation, and with awareness that my perspective has yet to be seasoned by persecution, I find Fr. Taft's conclusions accurate in part. Perhaps Tertullian and Clement are both alive and well within me. Yes, this world is not my home. And this world and its inhabitants were created by the Life-Giver and, consequently, bear His fingerprints. Seeking to see and celebrate those fingerprints connects me with God's present presence and, accordingly, causes me to be more fully present to the souls for whom Christ died. Yes, self-denial ("mortification") is implicit in the call to follow Christ. And self-denial, though strenuous, frees me from the sticky stuff of self-consciousness, increases within me the sacred stuff of God-consciousness, and fills me with an unspeakable joy. Yes, fasting detaches me from earthly things as it whispers reminders to me of Jesus' sacrifice. And fasting opens space in my soul for the amplification of God's love song.

Today's Reading: John 21:10–14

_____

_____

_____

_____

_____

_____

_____

_____

_____

_____

_____

_____

_____

DAY THIRTY-NINE

At the chief priests' and Pharisees' request, Pilate secured the tomb with a seal and soldiers (Matthew 27:62–66). Guards were positioned to keep the dead from the living. The rulers feared that the disciples might steal the body of Jesus, but the disciples were hiding behind locked doors in fear of the rulers (John 20:19). Even without any opposition, however, guarding tombs is a joyless job, as anyone who has ever sought to keep the past from the future can attest. After the Sabbath ended, Mary Magdalene, Joanna, Mary the mother of James, and Salome purchased spices, slept, and then left at dawn the next morning to visit the tomb.[1] Matthew recorded that,

> There was a violent earthquake, for an angel of the Lord came down from heaven and, going to the tomb, rolled back the stone and sat on it. His appearance was like lightning, and his clothes were white as snow. The guards were so afraid of him that they shook and became like dead men. (Matthew 28:2–4)

This was the second earthquake in three days for the guards. Add an angel and they were done!

Jesus was obviously gone before the stone was rolled away. His messenger was there to open the way in for the women, not the way out for the Savior. (As though a stone of any size could stop His love!) As this was a day for celebration, not subtlety, a less-than-camouflaged angel[2] glowed like lightning in front of the open tomb and said words that changed history. Inviting the women inside to see where Jesus had laid, the angel announced: "He is not here; he has risen, just as he said. . . . 'He has risen from the dead and is going ahead of you into Galilee. There you will see Him'" (Matthew 28:6–7).

> "If any have labored long in fasting, let him now receive his recompense. If any have wrought from the first hour, let him today receive his just reward. If any have come at the third hour, let him with thankfulness keep the feast. If any have arrived at the sixth hour, let him have no misgivings; because he shall in nowise be deprived therefore. If any have delayed until the ninth hour, let him draw near, fearing nothing. If any have tarried even until the eleventh hour, let him, also, be not alarmed at his tardiness; for the Lord, who is jealous of his honor, will accept the last even as the first; he gives rest unto him who comes at the eleventh hour, even as unto him who has wrought from the first hour. . . . And he shows mercy upon the last, and cares for the first; and to the one he gives, and upon the other he bestows gifts. And he both accepts the deeds, and welcomes the intention, and honors the acts and praises the offering."
>
> —SAINT JOHN CHRYSOSTOM (C. 347– 407), FROM HIS PASCHAL SERMON[3]

"Trembling and bewildered" (Mark 16:8), they "hurried away from the tomb, afraid yet filled with joy," and then, "suddenly..." (Matthew 28:8–9).

Consider slowly the angel's words: *He is not here. He is risen. Just as He said. He is risen from the dead. He is going ahead of you. And you will see Him.*

Oh the mysteries Jesus has uttered that will one day reveal themselves as miracles! Oh the ground on which God seemed as silent as the grave that will one day spring forth eternal life! Oh the times we assumed ourselves alone that will one day display that He had gone before us! The women waited days and we may wait decades, but just as Jesus said, we, too, will see Him one day.

Whereas guarding tombs is wearisome work, empty tombs are wondrous things. Not far from a bloodstained cross in Golgotha, one empty tomb brought hope to humanity.

Angels graced it (Mark 6:5).

Women were filled with joy at the sight of it (Matthew 28:8).

Peter ran to it (Luke 24:12).

John believed within it (John 20:8).

All of which was made possible because Jesus had conquered it!

Reflection

Place yourself in the position of the guards. What did they feel? See? Hear? Consider their assignment, that is, why they were placed to guard the tomb (Matthew 27:62–66). What options did they have after the angelic earthquake? Then read of their choice in Matthew 28:11–15 and ponder how many paid dearly for the guards' refusal to live and die for truth.

Today's Fast: Guarding Tombs

In today's reading, I stated that, "Guarding tombs is a joyless job, as anyone who has ever sought to keep the past from the future will attest." Are you weary of hiding the past from the future? In our readings, Christ's resurrection is just around the corner: do you believe in new life? We quote Easter's promise, "If anyone is in Christ, the new creation has come: the old has gone, the new is here!" (2 Corinthians 5:17). Yet we still permit shame to haunt our past.

Jesus did not merely dust me off and iron out a few of the more stubborn wrinkles in my life: He *saved* me because I was in desperate need of saving. I am alive only because He lives. Perhaps seven years after Jesus mercifully disrupted my atheistic existence, an old friend leaned in and whispered, "Okay, but we hung out together. I remember the things you said and did." I leaned in as well and in something close to a joyous shout replied, "So does my Jesus! He knows it all. And He has forgiven it all!"

Is shame standing watch over any dead things in your life? Jesus died to forgive you—follow His example and forgive yourself. Fast guarding that tomb. Let an earthquake or an angel roll away the stone so that you can see that *nothing is there anymore*. It is empty. Jesus conquered it. Jesus removed it. All that is there now is light and hope.

So rest, weary soldier. Jesus' empty tomb means that shame has no ground on which to stand.

On Lent

In Conclusion, part three: John H. Coe asserted that, "The soul must learn to love God just for Himself in such a manner that He, and not the need to be loved, is the center of all things."[4] Agreed. Lent, then, for this novice, most certainly is laden with great meaning: Lent is a concentrated opportunity to consciously and corporately fellowship with Christ in His suffering. And fellowship with Jesus—be it near His bloodstained feet on the cross or near His joy-brightened face at the wedding feast in Cana—is sweet indeed.

Today's Reading: John 21:15–19

_____

_____

_____

_____

_____

_____

_____

_____

_____

_____

_____

_____

DAY FORTY

Suddenly Jesus met them.
—MATTHEW 28:9

Would you think Him a vision? A dream? If the risen Christ suddenly appeared, would you stand or fall to your knees? Stay still or run to find a witness? I have rested with this image for decades since Jesus interrupted my life, but even more frequently since the oncologist said "cancer" a few years ago. To see Him: How can I describe how my very being aches to see Him? But then, perhaps no description is needed. Perhaps you ache too. I imagine His eyes being so loud that they drown out all words. I imagine being suspended in love, unprotected and unafraid, with His gaze more than enough to sustain me. Then, like the loveliest of music, the note dissipates . . . as a dog barks or the phone rings or a glass breaks and this world reminds me that I am still needed here, on the ground. And by faith I am comforted that my spirit still sees Jesus—"Christ in you, the hope of glory" (Colossians 1:27)—and that He is as present to me as He was to the first disciples.

Jesus died. His disciples heard His last words. They saw Him take his final breath. They witnessed soldiers piercing His side and testified to the "sudden flow of blood and water" it produced (John 19:33–35). They observed where He was buried. They mourned three days. Then suddenly, the risen Jesus stood before them! Jesus appeared to well over five hundred people (1 Corinthians 15:5–8) over a period of forty days (Acts 1:3). The Gospels record His appearances to grieving women at the tomb,[1] two disciples on the Emmaus road,[2] fearful and doubting disciples behind locked doors (John 20:19, 26–29), the Eleven at mealtime,[3] fish-less fishermen by the Sea of Galilee (John 21:1–14), and faithful followers gathered on a mountain for Jesus' closing commission and ascension.[4]

Jesus was not hiding, but His disciples struggled to identify Him. A few recognized Him by His words,[5] many by His wounds,[6] two by the breaking of bread (Luke 24:30–31), and a small boatful by the smell of fish.[7] We, too, struggle to recognize Jesus graveside, on long roads, behind locked doors, when hungry, and in empty seas. And so He appears, in His Word, in our pain, in communion, and through provision.

How must Jesus feel when His disciples recognize Him? When the fog of fear lifts and we behold His power? When the smog of self thins enough for us to realize that all He does, He does for love?

On Day One I stated, "Decrease is only holy when its destination is love." Jesus' decrease was holy. The author of Hebrews speaks of how Jesus endured the cross "for the joy set before Him" (Hebrews 12:2). That joy, my friend, was you and me and every soul on earth. In gratitude, we, too, like our Jesus, willingly take the path of decrease: not for decrease's sake, nor even for our sake. Like John the Baptist before us, we decrease so that Jesus can increase in and through us. And then one day, one glorious day, when our decrease is complete, we will stand with a multitude in the presence of our risen Savior and shout:

> Crown Him with many crowns, The Lamb upon His throne;
> Hark! How the heav'nly anthem drowns all music but its own!

Awake, my soul and sing of Him Who died for thee,
And hail Him as thy matchless King through all eternity.
Crown Him the Lord of love! Behold His hands and side—
Rich wounds, yet visible above, in beauty glorified.
No angel in the sky can fully bear that sight,
But downward bends His wond'ring eye at mysteries so bright.
Crown Him the Lord of life! Who triumphed o'er the grave,
Who rose victorious in the strife for those He came to save.
His glories now we sing, Who died, and rose on high,
Who died eternal life to bring, and lives that death may die.
Crown Him the Lord of heav'n! One with the Father known,
One with the Spirit through Him giv'n from yonder glorious
   throne,
To Thee be endless praise, for Thou for us hast died;
Be Thou, O Lord, through endless days adored and magnified.[8]

Reflection

Forty days ago you entered a journey of holy decrease. Our focus has been to "be duly awed by Christ's resurrection by being duly available to daily crucifixion." My personal prayer for you is that Christ's sacrifice is now clearer and that His resurrection is now dearer. Whether you experienced *40 Days of Decrease* during Lent or in another season to heighten your honor of Jesus as Redeemer, take time today to look back over this book and any notes you have made. What concepts stood out to you? Were there any areas in which a discrepancy was revealed between God's thoughts toward you and the thoughts you have toward yourself? In what ways

> "The more I considered Christianity, the more I found that while it has established a rule and order, the chief aim of that order was to give room for good things to run wild."
>
> —G. K. CHESTERTON
> (1874–1936)[9]

has the journey enriched your portrait of God? Then pause in gratitude to Jesus, your Mentor, for His holy decrease that was inspired by love.

Today's Fast: Fasting

Today, fast fasting and celebrate our risen Savior. Rejoice in His resurrection and anticipate His return. The past thirty-nine days of decrease have unsettled us, uncluttered us, and increased our capacity to see, serve, and celebrate Jesus. Add your voice today to the great cloud of witnesses that surrounds us (Hebrews 12:1). With the angel at the tomb, proclaim, "He is not here; He has risen!" (Matthew 28:6). With the women greeted by a stone that had already been rolled away, be filled with joy and hurry to tell others (Matthew 28:8). With the two along the Emmaus road, hear Jesus' voice, and let your heart burn within you (Luke 24:32). With Thomas, exclaim, "My Lord and my God!" (John 20:28). With the Eleven, assemble with others and ask God to open your mind to understand the Scriptures (Luke 24:45). With the heavenly host shout, "Holy, holy, holy is the Lord God Almighty, who was and is, and is to come" (Revelation 4:8). And with John pray, "Amen, Come, Lord Jesus" (Revelation 22:21).

> Christ has died.
> Christ has risen.
> Christ will come again.[10]

May we live in awe!

On Lent

This final sidebar is to be written by you as you continue taking your place in the history of Jesus' church. By any standards, honoring Jesus' death and resurrection is an ancient tradition dating back to the days of the Apostles (though as a forty-day Lenten journey its form solidified a few centuries later). I invite you to intentionally mentor your generation (and the next) toward living in gratitude for Christ's sacrifice and in awe of His resurrection. Below, write a brief letter to Jesus thanking Him for journeying cross-ward through death to bring you into eternal life.

Today's Reading: John 21:20–25

_____

_____

_____

_____

_____

_____

_____

_____

NOTES

PROLOGUE

1. Alicia Britt Chole, *Anonymous: Jesus' Hidden Years and Yours* (Nashville, TN: Thomas Nelson, 2006), 89–90.

INTRODUCTION

1. In Eastern Orthodox Churches, the forty days of Great Lent begin on a Monday and are inclusive of Sundays. The six weeks of Great Lent conclude on Palm Sunday when Holy Week begins. "Balancing the seven weeks of Lent and Holy Week, there follows after Easter a corresponding season of fifty days of thanksgiving, concluding with Pentecost." *The Lenten Triodion*, Service Books of the Orthodox Church (South Canaan, PA: St. Tikhon, 1994, 1977), 13–14.

2. For examples in the Scriptures of the use of ashes as a symbol of mourning, see 2 Samuel 13:19, Esther 4:1, Job 2:8, and Daniel 9:3.

3. Alexander Schmemann, *Great Lent*, rev. ed. (Crestwood, NY: St. Vladimir's Seminary Press, 1974), 31.

DAY ONE

1. Eugene Peterson, "Transparent Lives," *The Christian Century* 23, November 29, 2003: 23.
2. From The Center for Liturgy at St. Louis University, accessed December 15, 2014, http://www.liturgy.slu.edu/romanmissal/christ_has_died.html.
3. This first of three acclamations making up the Memorial Acclamation in the first English version of the *Roman Missal* has been described as more of a Latin adaptation than a Latin translation. As of 2008, the first acclamation of what is now called the Mystery of Faith reads, "Dying you destroyed our death. Rising you restored our life. Lord Jesus, come in glory." See http://content.ocp.org/shared/pdf/general/TL-NewRomanMissal-MysteryofFaith.pdf, accessed June 3, 2015.
4. OED Online, s. v. "sojourn, n.," accessed December 22, 2014, http://www.oed.com.georgefox.idm.oclc.org/view/Entry/184006?rskey=8IRiLR&result=1.
5. John H. Coe, "Resisting the Temptation of Moral Formation: Opening to Spiritual Formation in the Cross of the Spirit," *Journal of Spiritual Formation and Soul Care* 1, no. 1 (March 1, 2008): 77.
6. If you would prefer more or different passages to read, simply search online for Lenten daily readings. Here is a link to a user-friendly collection of daily readings from Disciples of Christ minister, Ken Collins: http://www.kencollins.com/texts/daily/1-lent.htm.

DAY TWO

1. Peterson, "Transparent Lives," 23.
2. *Apophthegmata Patrum*, Alphabetical Collection, Poemen 15, as quoted in Everett Ferguson, *Inheriting Wisdom: Readings for Today from Ancient Christian Writers* (Peabody, MA: Hendrickson Publishers, 2004), 52.
3. Dan B. Allender and Tremper Longman III, *The Cry of the Soul: How Our Emotions Reveal Our Deepest Questions about God* (Colorado Springs, CO: NavPress, 1994), 24.
4. Robert F. Taft, "Lent: A Meditation," *Worship* 57, no. 2 (March 1, 1983): 132.
5. See chapters 8–10 of St. Bernard of Clairvaux, *On the Love of God.* The entire text can be read online at the Christian Classics Ethereal Library, http://www.ccel.org/ccel/bernard/loving_god.

DAY THREE

1. Warnie Lewis, ed., *Letters of C. S. Lewis* (London: Geoffrey Bles, 1966), 285.
2. Chole, *Anonymous*, 113.
3. Carole C. Carlson, *Corrie Ten Boom, Her Life, Her Faith: A Biography* (Old Tappan, NJ: F.H. Revell Co., 1983), as cited in chapter 9 of Thomas E. Hollingsworth, *The Effective Christian*, 2001, http://www.theeffectivechristian.org/index.htm.
4. Mother Maria and Diokleia Kallistos, *The Lenten Triodion* (South Canaan, PA: Saint Tikhon's Seminary Press), 23.
5. William P. Saunders, "The Origins of Lent," *Catholic Herald*, March 2, 2006.
6. Nicholas V. Russo, "The Early History of Lent," *Lent Library* (Waco, TX: The Center for Christian Ethics at Baylor University, 2013), 19, http:/www.baylor.edu/content/services/document.php/193181.pdf.

DAY FOUR

1. Annie Dillard, *Teaching a Stone to Talk: Expeditions and Encounters* (New York: HarperPerennial, 1992), 43.
2. Also called the Sunday of Forgiveness, this is the last Sunday before the beginning of Great Lent in the Orthodox tradition.
3. Schmemann, *Great Lent*, 29–30.
4. Russo, "The Early History of Lent," 19.
5. Ibid.
6. John Paul Abdelsayed, "A History of the Great Lent," *Coptic Church Review* 31, no. 1 (March 1, 2010): 19.
7. Russo, "The Early History of Lent," 18; Abdelsayed, "A History of the Great Lent," 19.
8. Abdelsayed, "A History of the Great Lent," 22–23.
9. Nicholas V. Russo, "A Note on the Role of Secret Mark in the Search for the Origins of Lent," *Studia Liturgica* 37, no. 2 (January 1, 2007): 196; Abdelsayed, "A History of the Great Lent," 23.
10. Abdelsayed, "A History of the Great Lent," 22, quoting Origen: "They fast, therefore, who have lost the bridegroom; we having him with us cannot fast. Nor do we say that we relax the restraints of Christian abstinence; for we have

the forty days consecrated to fasting, we have the fourth and sixth days of the week, on which we fast solemnly."

11. Russo, "The Early History of Lent," 18.

12. Schmemann, *Great Lent*, 135.

DAY FIVE

1. See Isaiah 40:3 and Matthew 3:4.

2. Leonard I. Sweet, *The Well-Played Life: Why Pleasing God Doesn't Have to Be Such Hard Work* (Carol Stream, IL: Tyndale House Publishers, Inc., 2014), Kindle edition, 101–102.

3. John of the Cross, *The Collected Works of Saint John of the Cross*, trans. Kieran Kavanaugh and Otilio Rodriguez, rev. ed. (Washington, DC: ICS Publications, 1991), 370.

4. Abelard, *Sic et Non*, quoted in Burge, *Heloise and Abelard*, 54. As cited in Diana Butler Bass, *A People's History of Christianity: The Other Side of the Story* (New York: HarperOne, 2009), Kindle edition, loc. 1475.

5. Eusebius, *History of the Church*, vol. 5, chapter 24, no. 12., *New Advent*, http://www.newadvent.org/fathers/250105.htm.

6. Ibid., chapter 23, no. 2.

7. Ibid., chapter 23, no. 1. Emphasis mine.

DAY SIX

1. Since dates of antiquity are understandably difficult to assert with certainty, Throughout *40 Days of Decrease*, I have chosen to reference time between events, as there seems to be more scholarly agreement with regard to the general ordering of events than the precise dating of events. Johnston, Ellisen, and Cheney suggest the dates of December AD 29 for John's imprisonment and March AD 31 for John's beheading, hence my estimate of fifteen months. See Johnston M. Cheney and Stanley A. Ellisen, *Jesus Christ the Greatest Life: A Unique Blending of the Four Gospels*, Logos Edition (Eugene, OR: Paradise Publishing Inc., 1999), 47, 65.

2. See Matthew 14:3–12 and Mark 6:14–29.

3. C. H. Spurgeon, *The Saint and His Saviour: The Progress of the Soul in the Knowledge of Jesus* (1857; repr., London: Hodder and Stoughton, 1889), 419.

4. Gayle Erwin, *The Jesus Style* (Cathedral City, CA: Yahshua Publishing, 2011), Kindle edition, loc. 113.

5. C.H. Spurgeon, "The Pitifulness of the Lord the Comfort of the Afflicted," Bible Hub Online Bible Study Suite, accessed June 3, 2015, http://biblehub .com/sermons/auth/spurgeon/the_pitifulness_of_the_lord_the_comfort _of_the_afflicted.htm.

6. Ibid., chapter 24, no. 2.

7. As a side note, I found the excerpts from Bishop Polycrates's letter fascinating and wondered if they reflected second-century foreshadowing of The East-West Schism to come, and/or the transition away from Jewish customs.

DAY SEVEN

1. See Matthew 14:32 and John 6:21.

2. See Matthew 16:21, Mark 8:31, and Luke 9:21–22.

3. Dietrich Bonhoeffer, *The Cost of Discipleship* (New York: Touchstone, 1995), 88.

4. Walter A. Elwell and Philip Wesley Comfort, *Tyndale Bible Dictionary*, Tyndale Reference Library (Wheaton, IL: Tyndale House Publishers, 2001), 337.

5. Leonard Sweet, *I Am a Follower: The Way, Truth, and Life of Following Jesus* (Nashville, TN: Thomas Nelson, 2012), Kindle edition, 153.

6. Abdelsayed, "A History of the Great Lent," 32.

7. I first heard of Bridegroom Fasts through the teachings of Basilea Schlink, German intellectual, author, and founder of a Lutheran order called the Evangelical Sisterhood of Mary.

8. Eusebius, chapter 24, no. 13.

DAY EIGHT

1. Coe, "Resisting the Temptation of Moral Formation: Opening to Spiritual Formation in the Cross of the Spirit," 57.

2. Saunders, "The Origins of Lent."

3. Herman Lilienthal Lonsdale, *Lent, Past and Present: A Study of the Primitive Origin of Lent, Its Purpose and Usages* [facsimile] (New York, NY: Thomas Whittaker, 1895), 68.

4. Leah Payne, PhD, comments on *On the History of Lent*, essay by Alicia Britt Chole for CHTH 511 and CHTH 512/Christian History and Theology, George Fox University, August, 2013.

DAY NINE

1. Philip Yancey, *Disappointment with God: Three Questions No One Asks Aloud* (Grand Rapids: Zondervan, 1988), 200–201.
2. OED Online, s. v. "rationalism, n.," accessed December 22, 2014, http://www.oed.com.georgefox.idm.oclc.org/view/Entry/158504?redirectedFrom =rationalism.
3. Robert K. Merton, "Science, Technology and Society in Seventeenth-Century England," *Osiris*, 4. (1938):425–26, accessed August 1, 2014, http://links.jstor.org/sici?sici=0369–7827%281938%291%3A4 %3C360%3ASTASIS%3E2.0.CO%3B2-P.
4. Peter Homans, *The Ability to Mourn: Disillusionment and the Social Origins of Psychoanalysis* (Chicago: University of Chicago Press, 1989), 213–14.
5. Paul Stoller, "Rationality," in *Critical Terms for Religious Studies*, ed. Mark C. Taylor (Chicago: University of Chicago Press, 1998), 253.
6. Russo, "The Early History of Lent," 25.
7. Ibid., 24.
8. Ibid., 18–19.

DAY TEN

1. See Matthew 20:29–34, Mark 10:46–52, and Luke 18:35–43.
2. Leonard I. Sweet and Frank Viola, *Jesus Manifesto: Restoring the Supremacy and Sovereignty of Jesus Christ* (Nashville, TN: Thomas Nelson, 2010), Kindle edition, loc. 1630.
3. Gerald G. May, *The Dark Night of the Soul: A Psychiatrist Explores the Connection between Darkness and Spiritual Growth* (San Francisco: HarperSanFrancisco, 2004), 133.
4. Ibid., 132–133.
5. Maria and Kallistos, *Lenten Tradition*, 30.

DAY ELEVEN

1. Maria and Kallistos, *Lenten Tradition*, 235.
2. OED Online, s. v. "classism, n.," accessed December 23, 2014, http://www.oed
   .com.georgefox.idm.oclc.org/view/Entry/33906?redirectedFrom=classism.
3. Russo points out in "The Early History of Lent," 19, that in Athanasius's "first
   five letters (AD 329–333), [he] indicates that the 'holy fast' spans only the six
   days before Pascha, perhaps revealing that Lent had not yet been observed in
   Egypt. When he introduces the forty-day Lent in his sixth letter (AD 334), [he]
   continues to note the beginning of the more ancient six-day fast of 'the holy
   days of Pascha,' even though it is now part of the new six-week fast."
4. Saunders, "The Origins of Lent"; Schmemann, *Great Lent*, 136; Thomas J.
   Talley, *The Origins of the Liturgical Year*, 2nd ed. (Collegeville, MN: Pueblo Books
   Liturgical Press, 1986), 214; Abdelsayed, "A History of the Great Lent," 40.
5. Russo, "The Early History of Lent," 23.
6. Maria and Kallistos, *Lenten Tradition*, 30.
7. Russo, "The Early History of Lent," 20.
8. Talley, *Origins*, 214; Patricia M. Mann, "How Rituals Form and Transform:
   The Scrutiny Rite from Medieval to Modern Times" (PhD diss., The Catholic
   University of America, 2011), 50, http://aladinrc.wrlc.org/bitstream/handle
   /1961/9309/MANN_cua_0043A_10153display.pdf?sequence=1; Dominic
   E. Serra, "New Observations about the Scrutinies of the Elect in Early Roman
   Practice,"*Worship* 57, no. 2 (March 1, 1983): 519.
9. Schmemann, *Great Lent*, 136; Russo, "The Early History of Lent," 20.
10. Schmemann, *Great Lent*, 136.
11. Mann, "How Rituals Form and Transform: The Scrutiny Rite from Medieval
    to Modern Times," 120.

DAY TWELVE

1. Martin Luther King, Jr., "A Christmas Sermon on Peace," 1967, accessed
   December 4, 2014, http://www.ecoflourish.com/Primers/education/Christmas
   _Sermon.html.
2. Yes, I just quoted a Buddhist monk's musings on ecosystems. No, I am not
   remotely a Universalist. Please, do not send me letters of concern. All who

live, whether they acknowledge Jesus as God or not, are wonderfully saturated with God's fingerprints. We are all the work of His hands. Therefore, I believe that I can learn from everyone who lives, because everyone who lives was created by my God. Thich Nhat Hanh, "Interbeing," in *Seeing Systems: Peace, Justice, and Sustainability* (Portland, OR: Northwest Earth Institute, 2014), 18.

3. *It's a Wonderful Life*, directed by Frank Capra, Liberty Films (II), 1947.

4. For more on Karinthy's role in the Six Degrees of Separation theory, see Albert-Lázló Barabási, *Linked: How Everything Is Connected to Everything Else and What It Means for Business, Science, and Everyday Life* (New York: Basic Books, 2014), 25ff.

5. Abdelsayed, "A History of the Great Lent," 20; Schmemann, *Great Lent*, 136.

6. Saunders, "The Origins of Lent."

7. Ibid.

8. Russo, "The Early History of Lent," 20.

9. Schmemann, *Great Lent*, 136.

DAY THIRTEEN

1. See Matthew 26:12, Mark 14:8, and John 12:7.

2. The full text of Pliny's *Natural History* is available online from The Internet Archive, accessed June 3, 2015, https://archive.org/search.php?query=Pliny%20natural%20history.

3. Andrew Dalby, *Dangerous Tastes: The Story of Spices*, vol. 1 of *California Studies in Food and Culture* (Berkeley: University of California Press, 2000), 83–88.

4. Thomas Walsh's English translation of the anonymously penned Spanish poem "Soneta a Cristo Crucificado," often attributed to John of the Cross. *Hispanic Anthology: Poems Translated from the Spanish by English and North American Poets*, collected and arranged by Thomas Walsh (New York: G. P. Putnam's Sons, 1920), http://users.ipfw.edu/jehle/POESIA/ACRISTEN.HTM.

5. J. D. Douglas and N. Hillyer, *New Bible Dictionary*, 2nd ed. (Leicester: InterVarsity, 1982), 855.

DAY FOURTEEN

1. James Swanson, *Dictionary of Biblical Languages with Semantic Domains: Greek (New Testament)*, Logos edition (Oak Harbor, WA: Logos Research Systems, Inc., 1997).

2. See John 12:16.

3. *Lent with the Saints* (London: Catholic Truth Society, 2006), 18.

4. Stephen Hampton, "'Welcome Dear Feast of Lent': Rival Understandings of the Forty-Day Fast in Early Stuart England," *Journal of Theological Studies* 63, no. 2 (October 1, 2012): 623.

5. Ibid., 632.

6. Ibid., 623.

7. Lonsdale, *Lent, Past and Present*, 16, 30.

8. Saunders, writing for the *Catholic Herald*, spoke of the weight of Irenaeus's words: "The importance of the passage, nevertheless, remains that since the time of 'our forefathers'—always an expression for the apostles—a 40-day period of Lenten preparation existed. However, the actual practices and duration of Lent were still not homogeneous throughout the Church."

9. Eusebius, chapter 23, no. 1.

10. Russo, "The Early History of Lent," 18.

DAY FIFTEEN

1. May, *The Dark Night of the Soul*, 45.

2. Anthony Reading, *Hope and Despair: How Perceptions of the Future Shape Human Behavior* (Baltimore, MD: Johns Hopkins University Press, 2004), 17.

3. Rowan Williams, *The Wound of Knowledge: Christian Spirituality from the New Testament to St. John of the Cross*, 2nd rev. ed. (Cambridge, MA: Cowley Publications, 2003), 21.

4. C. S. Lewis, *The Chronicles of Narnia*, book 2, *The Lion, the Witch, and the Wardrobe* (New York: HarperCollins Publishers, 2003), 107.

5. Russo, "Secret Mark," 183, summarizes: "It was a long-held assumption among liturgical scholars that the post-Nicene emergence of a forty-day pre-paschal Lent owed its *origins* to the gradual backward extension of the primitive one- or two-day Easter fast of the kind known to Tertullian (*De ieiunio* 13–14)." See also Russo, "The Early History of Lent," 19, which states: "Accordingly, it was assumed that the forty-day Lent that we encounter almost everywhere by the mid-fourth century must have been the result of a gradual lengthening of the pre-Easter fast by adding days and weeks to the original one- or two-day observance."

6. Maria and Kallistos, *Lenten Tradition*, 29.

7. Abdelsayed, "A History of the Great Lent," 18.

8. Thomas Hopko, *The Lenten Spring: Readings for Great Lent* (Crestwood, NY: St. Vladimir's Seminary Press, 1998), 81; Lonsdale, 18, 33, 35.

9. For a modern example of this line of reasoning, consider Mann, "How Rituals Form," 50.

10. Russo, "Secret Mark," 74.

DAY SIXTEEN

1. Gerhard Kittel, Gerhard Friedrich, and Geoffrey William Bromiley, *Theological Dictionary of the New Testament* (Grand Rapids, MI: W. B. Eerdmans, 1985).

2. Yancey, *Disappointment with God*, 115.

3. Another frequently mentioned source was Thomas J. Talley. However, Talley's theory (how a post-theophany fast attached to Pascha to form Lent) was based in part upon Talley's confidence in the highly controversial Secret Mark. For a strong but respectful critique of that confidence that maintains the contribution of Talley to this subject, please see Nicholas V. Russo, "Secret Mark," 181–97.

4. E. Johnson, "From Three Weeks to Forty Days: Baptismal Preparation and the Origins of Lent," *Studia Liturgica* 20, no. 2 (January 1, 1990): 196.

5. Abdelsayed, "A History of the Great Lent," 18–19.

DAY SEVENTEEN

1. See also Luke 19:41 and John 2:15.

2. See also Mark 11:15 and John 2:15.

3. See also Matthew 21:12, Mark 11:17, and Luke 19:46.

4. Henri J. M. Nouwen, *Out of Solitude: Three Meditations on the Christian Life* (Notre Dame, IN: Ava Maria Press, 1974), 54.

5. Elmer L. Gray, "Money Changers," edited by Chad Brand et al., *Holman Illustrated Bible Dictionary* (Nashville, TN: Holman Bible Publishers, 2003), 1149.

6. OED Online, s. v. "apathy, n.," accessed December 26, 2014, http://www.oed.com.georgefox.idm.oclc.org /view/Entry/9052?redirectedFrom=apathy.

7. *Roget's 21st Century Thesaurus, Third Edition,* s. v. "apathy." Thesaurus.com, accessed Dec. 26, 2014, http://www.thesaurus.com/browse/apathy.

8. Alicia Britt Chole, "Week 32: The Discipline of Restraint," in *The 7th Year* (Rogersville, MO: Onewholeworld, Inc., 2011).

9. Informal conversation with Dr. Beth Grant, co-founder of Project Rescue, www.projectrescue.org.

10. Russo, "The Early History of Lent," 19.

DAY EIGHTEEN

1. See also Mark 11:13–14.

2. Robert B. Hughes and J. Carl Laney, *Tyndale Concise Bible Commentary,* The Tyndale Reference Library (Wheaton, IL: Tyndale House Publishers, 2001).

3. As an interesting aside, in his commentary, Matthew Henry points out that Jesus' curse reverses the very first blessing God gave: "God blessed them and said to them, 'Be fruitful.'" See Matthew Henry, "Genesis 1:28," *Matthew Henry's Commentary on the Whole Bible: Complete and Unabridged in One Volume* (Peabody, MA: Hendrickson, 1994, Logos).

4. See Matthew 21:21–22 and Mark 11:23–24.

5. H. L. Willmington, *Willmington's Bible Handbook* (Wheaton, IL: Tyndale House Publishers, 1997).

6. Craig S. Keener, *The IVP Bible Background Commentary: New Testament* (Downers Grove, IL: InterVarsity Press, 1993, Logos).

7. Traditional hymn by which Orthodox believers greet Lent on the Wednesday before Cheese-Fare Sunday. Quoted in Schmemann, *Great Lent,* 27.

8. Ibid., 25. For further consideration, please see Talley, *Origins,* 214; Robert B. Kruschwitz, "The Early History of Lent," in *Study Guides for Lent,* ed. Robert B. Kruschwitz (Waco, TX: The Center for Christian Ethics at Baylor University, 2013), 4, http://www.baylor.edu/content/services/document.php/193431. pdf; Russo, "The Early History of Lent," 20; Abdelsayed, "A History of the Great Lent," 20–23; Johnson, "From Three Weeks to Forty Days," 195; Schmemann, *Great Lent,* 135; and Maria and Kallistos, *Lenten Tradition,* 30–31. Additionally, for Russo's respectful evaluation of Talley's conclusions based upon Secret Mark, see Russo "The Early History of Lent," 21.

9. Schmemann, *Great Lent,* 14.

DAY NINETEEN

1. Alice Fryling, *Seeking God Together: An Introduction to Group Spiritual Direction* (Downer's Grove, IL: IVP Books, 2009), Kindle edition, 20, 22.
2. See also Mark 11:33 and Luke 20:8.

DAY TWENTY

1. George Kalantzis, "From the Porch to the Cross: Ancient Christian Approaches to Spiritual Formation," in *Life in the Spirit: Spiritual Formation in Theological Perspective*, ed. Jeffrey P. Greenman and George Kalantzis (Downers Grove, IL: IVP Academic, 2010), 81, accessed December 3, 2012, ATLA Religion Database with ATLASerials.
2. Walter A. Elwell and Philip Wesley Comfort, *Tyndale Bible Dictionary*, Tyndale Reference Library (Wheaton, IL: Tyndale House Publishers, 2001), 807; See Exodus 23:18, 34:25.
3. One of the most fascinating practices was, unfortunately, only mentioned in Lonsdale, *Lent, Past and Present*, 73–74, 120–121, without references through which more research could have been pursued. Lonsdale states that in the Lenten season, civil law "forbade all prosecution of men in criminal actions which might bring them to corporal punishment and torture;" lawsuits were postponed; "bodily punishment such as flogging and branding" were forbidden; and that "imperial indulgences [were] shown especially during this great week by the Emperors to all prisoners—criminals as well as debtors."
4. For a readable summary of Orthodox Lenten practice by week and focus, see Schmemann, *Great Lent*, 17–29. Also of interest is Hopko, *Lenten Spring*, 9.
5. For more on this contrast, consider Dale T. Irvin and Scott W. Sunquist, *History of the World Christian Movement: Earliest Christianity to 1453* (Maryknoll, NY: Orbis Books, 2001), loc. 8085 and 8520; Maria and Kallistos, *Lenten Tradition*, 15, 17; Schmemann, *Great Lent*, 137; and Abdelsayed, "A History of the Great Lent," 31–32.

DAY TWENTY-ONE

1. Johannes P. Louw and Eugene Albert Nida, *Greek-English Lexicon of the New Testament: Based on Semantic Domains* (New York: United Bible Societies, 1996), 320.

2. James Swanson, *Dictionary of Biblical Languages with Semantic Domains: Greek (New Testament)* (Oak Harbor, WA: Logos Research Systems, Inc., 1997).

3. Speaking of trouble, soon after Jesus described His heart as troubled (John 12:27), He told His disciples twice, "Do not let your hearts be troubled" (John 14:1, 27). Although "trouble" in all three verses is translated from ταράσσω (*tarassō*), "heart" is translated in John 12 from ψυχή (*psyche*), whereas "heart" in John 14 is translated from καρδία (*kardia*). Though interesting, the difference is not clarifying because both words can be used to describe one's inner self and thoughts. Context, however, is key. In John 12, Jesus was reaffirming His agonizing commitment to drink "this cup." The chapter headings in John 14 distract us, however, from what kind of "trouble" Jesus was referencing. At the Last Supper, Jesus told the disciples that He was leaving. Peter wanted to go, even if the "where" was death. Then Jesus said, "Will you really lay down your life for me? Very truly I tell you, before the rooster crows you will disown me three times! Do not let your heart be troubled. You believe in God; believe also in me. My Father's house has many rooms ..." (John 13:38–14:2). In other words, "Peter, don't let yourself be unnerved by the unknown. I'll bring you to where I'm going, even after you fail."

4. Yancey, *Disappointment with God*, 192.

5. Differing fasting practices are consistently listed as among the lesser, but still contributing, factors to the Great Schism of 1054.

6. For a fascinating discussion of early-reformation response to fasting (inclusive of quotes from Luther and Calvin on the subject of fasting) in Stuart England, see Stephen Hampton, "'Welcome Dear Feast of Lent,'" 608–648.

7. Saunders, "The Origins of Lent."

8. Cited in Ibid.

9. Contrast Lonsdale, *Lent, Past and Present*, 44, on grace extended by St. Chrysostom to those who could not keep the fast with the Sausage Incident during Lent of 1522 in Lindberg, 161.

10. Maria and Kallistos, *Lenten Tradition*, 16.

11. Ibid., 100.

12. In the words of St. John Climacus from *The Ladder of Paradise*, Step 7, as quoted by Maria and Kallistos, *Lenten Tradition*, 22.

13. St. Chrysostom as quoted in Lonsdale, *Lent, Past and Present*, 110.

DAY TWENTY-TWO

1. For further study, see Matthew 3:17, Mark 1:11, and Luke 3:21–22 for Jesus' baptism; Matthew 17:5, Mark 9:7, and Luke 9:35 for the Transfiguration; and John 12:28 for prior to the Last Supper. At the Transfiguration, God's voice came from a cloud. At the baptism and prior to the Last Supper, God's voice came from heaven.

2. Swanson, *Dictionary of Biblical Languages.*

3. Scripture does not record whether or not John also heard God's voice at Jesus' baptism. When John gives his testimony in John 1:32, he mentions the Spirit descending upon Jesus but not God's voice from the heavens as evidence that Jesus was "the Son of God."

4. James Davison Hunter, *To Change the World: The Irony, Tragedy, and Possibility of Christianity in the Late Modern World* (New York: Oxford University Press USA, 2010), Kindle edition, 154.

5. Schmemann, *Great Lent,* 96.

6. Maria and Kallistos, *Lenten Tradition,* 235.

7. Ibid., 17.

DAY TWENTY-THREE

1. Consider Hebrews 4:15, which assures us that, "We do not have a high priest who is unable to sympathize with our weaknesses, but we have one who has been tempted in every way, just as we are—yet he did not sin."

2. See Matthew 26:14–16, Mark 14:10–11, and Luke 22:3–6.

3. See Matthew 26:69–75, Mark 14:66–72, Luke 22:55–62, and John 18:16–18, 25–27.

4. See Matthew 26:35 and Mark 14:31.

5. Henri J. M. Nouwen, *A Cry for Mercy: Prayers from the Genesee,* Image Edition (New York: DoubleDay, 1981, 2002), 43.

6. Marianne Meye Thompson, "Turning and Returning to God: Reflections on the Lectionary Texts for Lent," *Interpretation* 64, no. 1 (January 1, 2010): 6.

7. Abdelsayed, "A History of the Great Lent," 26.

8. Pope Francis, March 5, 2014 Ash Wednesday Mass, as reported by Cindy Wooden for the Catholic News Service, accessed April 27, 2015, http://www.catholicnews.com/data/stories/cns/1400924.htm.

DAY TWENTY-FOUR

1. In the course of writing this book, I was delighted to discover that *The Message* version of the Bible translates John 14:31 similarly: "Get up. Let's go. It's time to leave here."
2. Sweet, *I Am a Follower*, Kindle edition, 153, loc. 2627–2634.
3. See also Matthew 16:24, Mark 8:34–35, and Luke 9:23.
4. See also Mark 8:34–37 and Luke 9:23–25.
5. Swanson, *Dictionary of Biblical Languages*.
6. Received via e-mail on August 6, 2013. Mark Bradshaw grew up in a Pentecostal tradition, and as an adult joined the Orthodox Church.

DAY TWENTY-FIVE

1. Avraham Negev, *The Archaeological Encyclopedia of the Holy Land* (New York: Prentice Hall Press, 1990).
2. See Luke 13:19, John 18:26, and John 19:41 for other occurrences of κῆπος (*kēpos*).
3. Josephus asserts that Titus's troops encamped in the Mount of Olives and "cut down all the fruit trees that lay between them and the wall of the city." Flavius Josephus, *The Complete Works*, trans. William Whiston. Nelson's Super Value Series (Nashville TN: T. Nelson Publishers, 1998), 842.
4. See Luke 22:39 and John 18:2.
5. Swanson, *Dictionary of Biblical Languages*.
6. Conversely, if we downgrade Jesus' sacrifice from "The Way" to "an available option," we simultaneously call Father God's character into question, for what father—let alone a heavenly one—would 1) lie in the face of such love, and 2) allow his child to experience such horrors if another means to accomplish the same end existed?
7. Gerhard Ludwig Müller and Albrecht Schönherr, eds., *Ethics*, vol. 6 of *Dietrich Bonhoeffer Works*, English-language edition (Minneapolis: Fortress Press, 1996–2014).
8. Though spoken in the context of sharing faith with others, Julian's wisdom is also true of sharing life with God. Larry S. Julian, *God Is My Coach: A Business Leader's Guide to Finding Clarity in an Uncertain World*, 1st ed. (New York: Center Street, 2009), loc. 998.

9. "Emotions are not truth's vocal twin, and feelings are not the litmus test for reality. Our emotions and feelings are simply reactions to our environment, circumstances, and perceptions. By nature they are followers, and we place our souls in danger when we require them to take the lead." *Chole, Anonymous*, 73.

10. Received via e-mail on August 6, 2013. Mark Bradshaw grew up in a Pentecostal tradition, and as an adult joined the Orthodox Church.

DAY TWENTY-SIX

1. Swanson, *Dictionary of Biblical Languages*.

2. Thomas Merton, *No Man Is an Island*, Harvest/HBJ ed. (New York: Harcourt, 1983), 237.

3. Yes, this is a nod to *Lord of the Rings*. #LOTRfan

4. Saint John Chrysostom, "The Paschal Sermon," Orthodox Church in America, accessed July 25, 2013, http://oca.org/fs/sermons/the-paschal -sermon.

5. Received via e-mail on August 6, 2013. Mark Bradshaw grew up in a Pentecostal tradition, and as an adult joined the Orthodox Church.

DAY TWENTY-SEVEN

1. See also Matthew 20:13 and 22:12.

2. Gerhard Kittel, Gerhard Friedrich, and Geoffrey William Bromiley, *Theological Dictionary of the New Testament* (Grand Rapids, MI: W.B. Eerdmans, 1985), 265.

3. Frank C. Laubach, *Learning the Vocabulary of God: A Spiritual Diary* (Mansfield Centre, CT: Martino Publishing, 2012), 17.

4. Maria and Kallistos, *Lenten Tradition*, 23. See also Robin M. Jensen, "Ashes, Shadows, and Crosses: Visualizing Lent," *Interpretation* 64, no. 1 (January 1, 2020): 18.

5. Ibid., 19.

6. Father Lewis Hejna of Imaculate Conception, interview by author, Springfield, Missouri, July 23, 2013.

DAY TWENTY-EIGHT

1. Alicia Britt Chole, "Week 33: The Discipline of Restraint," in *The 7th Year* (Rogersville, MO: Onewholeworld, Inc., 2011).
2. George MacDonald, *The Hope of the Gospel* (Charleston, SC: CreateSpace Independent Publishing Platform, 2013), 18.
3. Chole, "Week 32."
4. For further study, see Luke 22:53 and John 7:30, 12:27, 13:1, 17:1.
5. For further study, see Matthew 20:22, 26:27, 39, 42; Mark 10:38; 14:36; Luke 22:20, 42; and John 18:11.
6. John 2:1–11. Yes, technically the miracle occurred somewhere between the water jars and the cups. (Work with me here.)
7. OED Online, s. v. "abstinence, n.," accessed April 27, 2015, http://www.oed .com.georgefox.idm.oclc.org/view/Entry/752?redirectedFrom=abstinence.
8. *Lent with the Saints*, 64.
9. As quoted in Lonsdale, *Lenten Tradition*, 76–77. The original source was not cited and I was unable to locate it.

DAY TWENTY-NINE

1. For further study, see John 18:12–13, 19–23.
2. For further study, see Matthew 26:57, Mark 14:53, and John 18:24.
3. For further study, see Matthew 27:11, Mark 15:1, Luke 23:1, and John 18:13–14, 24, 28.
4. For further study, see Luke 23:7–11.
5. For further study, see Luke 23:11.
6. Albeit a sloppy paraphrase that was entirely misunderstood, Jesus did say this to the religious leaders in Jerusalem as recorded in John 2:19. John explained Jesus' meaning: "But the temple he had spoken of was his body. After he was raised from the dead, his disciples recalled what he had said" (John 2:21–22).
7. See also Mark 14:57–58.
8. See also Mark 14:61–63 and Luke 22:67–71.
9. Jesus actually taught just the opposite. For further study, see Matthew 17:27, 22:21.

10. For further study, see John 18:37.

11. Jesus made it clear that His kingdom was not of this earth. For further study, see John 18:36.

12. Philo, *On The Embassy of Gauis* Book XXXVIII, 299–305, accessed April 21, 2015, http://www.earlychristianwritings.com/yonge/book40.html.

13. Thomas Merton, *A Doubleday Image Book*, vol. D183, *Life and Holiness* (New York: Image Books, 1963), 119.

DAY THIRTY

1. Peter's story of denial can be found in Matthew 26:69–75, Mark 14:66–72, Luke 22:54–62, and John 18:15–18, 25–27.

2. See Matthew 26:52, Luke 22:51, and John 18:11.

3. See Matthew 26:56, 58; Mark 14:50, 66; Luke 22:54–55; and John 18:15–16, 18.

4. See Matthew 26:69–74, Mark 14:66–71, Luke 22:56–60, and John 18:17, 25–27.

5. See also Matthew 26:50.

6. Thomas Keating, *Fruits and Gifts of the Spirit* (New York: Lantern Books, 2000), 67.

7. Alicia Britt Chole, "Week 48: On Sabbath Rest and Prayer Retreats," in *The 7th Year*, (Rogersville, MO: Onewholeworld, Inc., 2011).

8. Maria and Kallistos, *Lenten Tradition*, 25, explain of this Orthodox practice that, "The abstinence of married couples, then, has as its aim not the suppression but the purification of sexuality. Such abstinence, practiced 'with mutual consent for a time' has always the positive aim, 'that you may give yourselves to fasting and prayer' (1 Cor. 7:5). Self-restraint, so far from indicating a dualist depreciation of the body, serves on the contrary to confer upon the sexual side of marriage a spiritual dimension which might otherwise be absent."

9. Hopko, *Lenten Spring*, 95.

10. Lonsdale, *Lent, Past and Present*, 71–73.

11. Maria and Kallistos, *Lenten Tradition*, 23. See also Jensen, "Ashes, Shadows, and Crosses," 30.

12. *Lent with the Saints*, 62.

DAY THIRTY-ONE

1. OED Online, s. v. "violent, adj., n., and adv.," accessed April 23, 2015, http://www.oed.com.georgefox.idm.oclc.org/view/Entry/223641?rskey=CtxB5j&result=1&isAdvanced=false.

2. OED Online, s. v. "mockery, n.," accessed April 23, 2015, http://www.oed.com.georgefox.idm.oclc.org/view/Entry/120540?redirectedFrom=mockery.

3. Ignatius, *The Spiritual Exercises of St. Ignatius* (New York: Doubleday, 1989, 1964), 54.

4. Yancey, *Disappointment with God*, 118.

5. See Matthew 26:67–68, Mark 14:65, and Luke 22:63–65.

6. See Matthew 27:26–30, Mark 15:15–20, and John 19:1–3.

7. Mann mentions Christian Initiation as part of a dissertation on the history of the Scrutinies. Because of space, I have chosen not to address the Scrutinies as a distinct practice in this summary. For more information on the scrutiny of paschal baptismal candidates please see Mann, "How Rituals Form"; Charles W. Gusmer, "The Purpose of the Scrutinies: An Insight from the Ignatian Exercises," *Worship* 65, no. 2 (October 1, 2012): 125–26; and Serra, "New Observations," 518, 521.

8. Today, in the Catholic Church, Christian Initiation is known as RCIA: The Rites of Christian Initiation for Adults.

9. Though the current rites are less exacting, the Catholic Church still practices a paschal Rite of Christian Initiation, as evidenced in the 1988 Vatican-issued circular letter *Paschalis Solemnitatis*. According to Servite Priest Fr. John M. Huels, this letter points out "the centrality of the rite of Christian initiation during the paschal season of Lent/Easter, and this emphasis on initiation recurs repeatedly in the document. See John M. Huels, "Chronicle: Preparing and Celebrating the Paschal Feasts," *Worship* 61, no. 2 (March 1, 1987): 73.

10. Mann, "How Rituals Form," 116, 123–24. Also of note, is the following from Mann: "The purpose, according to Augustine [AD 354–430], was to grind the *competentes* as grain into flour for making that bread he called the *corpus mysticum Christi* which he thought of as both church and Eucharist." Mann, "How Rituals Form," 135.

DAY THIRTY-TWO

1. See Matthew 27:23; Luke 23:4, 14, 22; and John 18:38, 19:4.
2. See Matthew 27:15–18, 20–21; Mark 15:9–12, 15; Luke 23:18–20, 25; and John 18:39–40.
3. See Luke 23:16, 22 and John 19:1.
4. See Matthew 27:22–23, Mark 15:12–14, and John 19:13–15.
5. Though Luke twice mentions Pilate's offer to punish and release Jesus, he does not specify when the flogging occurred.
6. Martin Hengel, *Crucifixion in the Ancient World and the Folly of the Message of the Cross*, American ed. (Philadelphia: Fortress Press, 1977), 29.
7. The exact number of lashes in Roman floggings varied, according to Dr. Vassilios Tzaferis, who said, "Although the number of strokes imposed was not fixed, care was taken not to kill the victim." Vassilios Tzaferis, "The Archaeological Evidence," Biblical Archaeological Society, accessed April 23, 2015, http://www.biblicalarchaeology.org/daily/biblical-topics/crucifixion/a-tomb-in-jerusalem-reveals-the-history-of-crucifixion-and-roman-crucifixion-methods/. Originally published as "Crucifixion—The Archaeological Evidence," *Biblical Archaeological Review* 11, no. 1 (January–February 1985): 44–53.
8. Hengel, *Crucifixion*, 31–32.
9. Robert Lowry, "Nothing but the Blood," 1887. Public Domain.
10. C. H. Spurgeon, "3 June: Philippians 2:8," *Evening by Evening* (London: Passmore and Alabaster, 1868), 155.
11. John 1:29, 36.
12. Schmemann, *Great Lent*, 29–30.
13. Huels, "Chronicle," 74; see also Jensen, "Ashes, Shadows, and Crosses," 30.
14. Jensen, "Ashes, Shadows, and Crosses," 30.
15. Ibid., 32.

DAY THIRTY-THREE

1. Of the traditionally commemorated fourteen Stations of the Cross, five (3, 4, 6, 7, and 9) are based upon noncanonical sources and legend. In 1991, on Good Friday, Pope John Paul II released a version of the Stations of the Cross, based entirely upon Scripture, that can be read online here: http://www.usccb.org

/prayer-and-worship/prayers-and-devotions/stations-of-the-cross/scriptural
-stations-of-the-cross.cfm. Understandably, Christian traditions have focused
upon different aspects of Jesus' suffering through the centuries. Personally,
I have been very grateful for the portrayal of Christ's suffering at Canaan
in the Desert in Phoenix, Arizona, on eight plaster reliefs depicting Jesus at
Gethsemane, before Pilate, flogged, crowned with thorns, carrying the cross,
crucified, buried, and resurrected.

2. Tzaferis, "Archaeological Evidence."

3. See Matthew 27:37, Mark 15:26, Luke 23:38, and John 19:19–22.

4. See Matthew 27:35, Mark 15:24, Luke 23:33, and John 19:18.

5. Tzaferis, "Archaeological Evidence."

6. Ibid.

7. Hengel, *Crucifixion*, 25.

8. Yancey, *Disappointment with God*, 185–186.

9. As a personal side note, my husband, Dr. Barry Jay Chole, had the privilege
of participating in an archeological dig in Capernaum under Dr. Tzaferis's
direction in 1984.

10. In 1968, archeologists had their first opportunity to study a victim of Roman
crucifixion via the discovered remains of a Jewish twenty-four- to twenty-
eight-year-old man of a wealthy family, who was convicted of political crimes
against Rome sometime before AD 70 and crucified just outside Jerusalem as
evidenced by his right heel bone, which was pierced by a nail that was initially
thought to be 7 inches in length. Like Jesus, scholars suggest that this man
was "given" a small point to sit upon during crucifixion. Dr. Tzaferis's initial
conclusions, which were largely based upon the findings of the medical team
under the direction of Dr. Nico Haas (specifically regarding the positioning
of the man's feet and legs, length of the nail—which was more accurately 4.5
inches—the structure of the man's face, and the meaning of scratches found in
the bones), were later refined by Dr. Hershel Shanks in "Scholars' Corner: New
Analysis of the Crucified Man," Biblical Archeology Society, accessed April 24,
2015, http://www.biblicalarchaeology.org/daily/biblical-topics/crucifixion
/roman-crucifixion-methods-reveal-the-history-of-crucifixion/. Originally
published as "New Analysis of the Crucified Man," *Biblical Archaeology Review*
11, no. 6 (November/December 1985).

11. Tzaferis, "Archaeological Evidence."

12. Robert Robinson, "Come Thou Fount," 1757, public domain.

13. Abdelsayed, "A History of the Great Lent," 18.

14. Pope Leo the Great (d. 461) in a homily still used today for breviary lessons on the first Sunday of Lent, as quoted in Alphonse E. Westhoff, "Parish Lenten Program," *Worship* 33, no. 3 (February 1, 1959): 177.

DAY THIRTY-FOUR

1. According to Chabad.org, an Orthodox Jewish website, "The hour has a special meaning in Jewish law. 'The third hour of the day' doesn't mean 3:00 a.m., or three sixty-minute hours after sunrise. Rather, an hour in *halacha* is calculated by taking the total time of daylight of a particular day, from sunrise until sunset, and dividing it into twelve equal parts. A *halachic* hour is thus known as a *sha'ah zemanit*, or proportional hour, and varies by the season and even by the day. For example, on a day when the sun rises at 5 a.m. and sets at 7:30 p.m., one *sha'ah zemanit*, or proportional hour, will be 72.5 minutes long. The third hour of the day will come to a close at 8:37:30 a.m. This information is important because many observances in Jewish law are performed at specific times during the day. The calculation of these halachic times, known as *zmanim* ("times"), depends on the length of the daylight hours in that locale." http://www.chabad.org/library/article_cdo/aid/526872/jewish/Hours.htm.

2. Timothy Murphy, "Address to the Manger," *First Things* no. 208 (December 2010): 46. ATLA Religion Database with ATLASerials, EBSCOhost (accessed April 25, 2015).

3. See also Mark 15:29.

4. Matthew 27:47. See also Mark 15:35.

5. Matthew 27:49. See also Mark 15:36.

6. Matthew 27:48. See also Mark 15:36.

7. Matthew 27:41–43. See also Mark 15:31–32 and Luke 23:35.

8. See Matthew 4:1–11, Mark 1:12–13, and Luke 4:1–13.

9. *Lent with the Saints*, 37.

10. St. John Climacus (AD 525–606), *The Ladder of Divine Ascent*, step 7. As quoted in Hopko, *Lenten Spring*, 13–14.

11. Henri Nouwen, *Show Me the Way* (New York: Crossroad, 1992), 174.

12. Carolyn J. Sharp, "Preaching the Prophets for Lent." *Journal for Preachers* 35, no. 2 (January 1, 2012): 22.

DAY THIRTY-FIVE

1. Matthew 27:38. See also Mark 15:27, Luke 23:33, and John 19:18.
2. Mark 15:32. See also Matthew 27:44.
3. Luke 23:44–45, NASB. See also Matthew 27:44 and Mark 15:33.
4. See Matthew 27:50, Mark 15:37, Luke 23:46, and John 19:30.
5. See also Mark 15:38 and Luke 23:45.
6. Gregory of Nazianzus, "The Oration on Holy Baptism," Oration 40:13, Jan. 6, 381. Accessed May 4, 2015, http://www.newadvent.org/fathers/310240.htm.
7. See Matthew 27:55–56 and Mark 15:40–41 and note that Matthew and Mark mentioned in this group the named women who John 19:25–27 positioned closer to the cross.
8. Luke 23:48 states that, "When all the people who had gathered to witness this sight saw what took place, they beat their breasts and went away," from which I conclude that the rulers also departed following Jesus' death.
9. In John 19:32–33, we read that the soldiers broke the robbers' legs, which was done to hasten death. "But when they came to Jesus and found that he was already dead, they did not break his legs."
10. See also Mark 15:39 and Luke 23:47.
11. John 19:30.
12. Benedict XVI, "Message of His Holiness Benedict XVI for Lent 2012." The Vatican, accessed June 3, 2015, http://w2.vatican.va/content/benedict-xvi/en/messages/lent/documents/hf_ben-xvi_mes_20111103_lent-2012.html.
13. Kevin Emmert, "Resting in the Work of God: The Forgotten Spiritual Discipline," *Christianity Today* 56, no. 3 (March 1, 2012): 26.
14. Lewis.

DAY THIRTY-SIX

1. Today's reading is largely based upon a devotional I wrote for my first, now out-of-print, book. Alicia Britt Chole, *Pure Joy: Words of Encouragement and Hope* (Nashville, TN: J. Countryman, 2003), 169–70.

2. See Matthew 27:57–60, Mark 15:42–46, Luke 23:50–55, and John 19:38–42.

3. Mark Davis, "Matthew 27:57–66," *Interpretation* 60, no. 1 (January 1, 2006): 76–77.

4. Neil Azevedo, "Annas (to Caiaphas); Barabbas (a Zealot's prayer); Pontius Pilate; Simon of Cyrene; Joseph of Arimathea; Nicodemus." *First Things* no. 101 (March 2000): 15. http://www.firstthings.com/article/2000/03/poetry-41.

5. Taft, "Lent," 132.

6. Ibid., 124.

DAY THIRTY-SEVEN

1. Whereas Matthew 27:56 identifies her as "Mary the mother of James and Joseph," later, in 27:61, Matthew refers to her as "the other Mary." Mark 15:40 refers to her as "Mary the mother of James the younger and of Joseph, and Salome," and Mark 16:47 simply calls her "Mary the mother of James, and Salome." History often (but not always) identifies her as the mother of James son of Alphaeus (Matthew 10:3), also known as James the Less.

2. See Matthew 27:62, Mark 15:42, Luke 23:54, and John 19:42.

3. *Apophthegmata Patrum*, Alphabetical Collection, Poemen 15, as quoted in Everett Ferguson, *Inheriting Wisdom: Readings for Today from Ancient Christian Writers* (Peabody, MA: Hendrickson Publishers, 2004), 231.

4. See note on Day Thirty-Four from Chabad.org.

5. Note the mention of a "special Sabbath" following Preparation Day in John 19:31.

6. Sean Kinsella, "Preparation Day," *Anglican Theological Review* 80, no. 3 (June 1, 1998): 395.

7. Brother Lawrence and Frank Laubach, *Practicing His Presence* (Auburn, ME: Christian Books, 1973), 82.

8. Taft, "Lent," 123.

9. Allan Menzies, ed., *The Writings of the Fathers down to AD 32*, vol. 3, *Latin Christianity: Its Founder, Tertullian* (Grand Rapids, MI: Wm. B. Eerdmans, 2009), 101, Christian Classics Ethereal Library, http://www.ccel.org/ccel/schaff/anf03.i.html.

10. Roger E. Olson, *The Story of Christian Theology: Twenty Centuries of Tradition and Reform* (Downers Grove, IL: IVP Academic, 1999), 87.

DAY THIRTY-EIGHT

1. See Acts 2:30–33, Ephesians 4:7–10, Colossians 2:13–17, and 1 Peter 3:18–22.
2. Today's reading is largely based upon a devotional I wrote for my second, now out-of-print book. Alicia Britt Chole, *Sitting in God's Sunshine, Resting in His Love* (Nashville, TN: J. Countryman, 2005), 150–54.
3. Joshua Heschel, *The Sabbath: Its Meaning for Modern Man* (New York: Farrar, Straus and Giroux, 2005), 14.
4. A. J. Swoboda, *"Developing a Thriving Community"* (lecture, George Fox Evangelical Seminary, Cannon Beach, OR, March 7, 2014).

DAY THIRTY-NINE

1. The women's names were compiled from all the accounts: Matthew 28:1, Mark 16:1, and Luke 24:10.
2. Whereas Matthew and Mark mention one angel, Luke and John mention two. Additionally, Matthew, Mark, and Luke speak of Jesus appearing to the women, whereas John attends more specifically to Mary Magdalene's story.
3. Saint John Chrysostom, "The Paschal Sermon." Orthodox Church in America, accessed June 4, 2015, http://oca.org/fs/sermons/the-paschal-sermon.
4. John H. Coe, "Musings on the Dark Night of the Soul: Insight from St. John of the Cross on Developmental Spirituality," *Journal of Psychology and Theology* 28, no. 4 (2000): 295.

DAY FORTY

1. See Matthew 28:9–10, Mark 16:9, and John 20:14–17.
2. See Mark 16:12 and Luke 24:13–32.
3. See Mark 16:14 and Luke 24:36–43.
4. See Matthew 28:16–20 and Luke 24:50–53.
5. See Matthew 28:9, Luke 24:32, and John 20:16.
6. See Luke 24:38–40 and John 20:20, 27–28.
7. See Luke 24:42–43 and John 21:6–7.
8. Mathew Bridges, "Crown Him with Many Crowns," 1851, public domain.
9. G. K. Chesterton, *Orthodoxy* (New Jersey: J.P. Piper Books, 2014), 99.

10. This first of three acclamations making up the Memorial Acclamation in the first English version of the *Roman Missal* has been described as more of a Latin adaption than a Latin translation. As of 2008, the first acclamation of what is now called the Mystery of Faith reads, "Dying you destroyed our death. Rising you restored our life. Lord Jesus, come in glory." See http://content.ocp.org/shared/pdf/general/TL-NewRomanMissal-MysteryofFaith.pdf.

ABOUT THE AUTHOR

Alicia Britt Chole has a doctor of ministry in leadership and spiritual formation from George Fox Evangelical Seminary and serves as the founding director of Leadership Investment Intensives (www.leadershipii.com), a nonprofit devoted to spiritually investing in the lives and legacies of leaders in the marketplace and the church. A captivating communicator, seasoned mentor, and gifted writer, Alicia speaks internationally and has authored several books including *Anonymous: Jesus' Hidden Years and Yours,* which is highly regarded by leaders around the world. In a culture obsessed with fame, Alicia brings ancient truth to life.

Alicia lives with her husband, their three amazing children (all Choles through the miracle of adoption), four somewhat-less-than-amazing dogs, one truly strange cat, and eight confused chickens off of a dirt road in a country home devoted to writing and reflection.

Among her favorite things are thunderstorms, pianos in empty rooms, organic hot tea, and anything with jalapenos. To connect with Alicia, visit **www.aliciachole.com** and **@aliciachole**.

ALSO AVAILABLE FROM
ALICIA BRITT CHOLE

9780718076603-A